IN MEMORY
OF THE MICHELIN EMPLOYEES
AND WORKMEN WHO DIED GLORIOUSLY
FOR THEIR COUNTRY.

RHEIMS

AND THE BATTLES FOR ITS POSSESSION.

On July 6th, 1919, the President of the French Republic conferred the **Croix de la Légion d'Honneur** *on Rheims (fastening it personally on the City Arms), with the following* **"citation"** *:—*

"Martyred city, destroyed by an infuriated enemy, powerless to hold it.

"Sublime population who, like the Municipal Authorities—models of devotion to duty and despising all danger—gave proof of magnificent courage, by remaining more than three years under the constant menace of the enemy's attacks, and by leaving their homes only when ordered to do so.

"Inspired by the example of the heroic French maid of venerated memory, whose statue stands in the heart of the city, showed unshakeable faith in the future of France (Croix de Guerre)."

RHEIMS, AS SEEN FROM THE GERMAN LINES

(Photograph found on a German prisoner)

RHEIMS

POLITICAL HISTORY

Rheims is one of the oldest towns in France, so old that legendary accounts, in an endeavour to outdo one another, carry back its foundation sometimes to 1440 B.C. after the Flood, sometimes to the siege of Troy. Lying at the intersection of the natural routes between Belgium and Burgundy, and between the Parisian basin and Lorraine, *i.e.* between political districts that long remained different in character, and regions having different commercial resources, it was at one and the same time the "*oppidum*" and *market-town*. Its military and commercial position destined it early to be a great city.

It probably takes its name from the tribe of the *Remi*, who occupied almost the whole territory now forming the "*départements*" of the Marne and the Ardennes, and who were clients of the *Suessiones* (Soissons) before the Roman conquest. It was already a prosperous town, under the name of "*Durocortorum*," when Cæsar conquered Gaul. It freed itself from the yoke of the *Suessiones* by accepting the Roman domination. When the Belgians revolted in 57 B.C., the *Remi* remained faithful to Cæsar and received the title of "*friends of the Roman people*." Neither did they take any part in the general revolt of Gaul in 52 B.C. Under the Empire, Rheims was, with Trèves, one of the great centres of Latin culture in "*Gallia Belgica*." On becoming a federated city, it retained its institutions and senate. A favourite residence of the Roman Governors, Rheims was embellished with sumptuous villas and magnificent monuments, and soon became one of the most prosperous towns in Gaul. At the beginning of the Germanic invasions Rheims drew in its borders and became a military town. Under *Diocletian* it was the capital of *Belgica Secunda*.

According to tradition, Christianity was first preached in Rheims by St. Sixtus and St. Sinirus, the first bishops of the city. However that may be, Christianity was firmly established there as early as the 3rd century. A bishop of Rheims was present at the Council of Arles in 314. The conversion of several great Roman personages (amongst others, the *Consul Jovinus*—see p. 118) favoured the progress of the Christian religion.

In the 5th century, when Rome, otherwise occupied, was unable to hold back the barbarians, invasions interfered with the development of the city. The Frankish conquest marked the beginning of a new period of prosperity. In 486, after the victory of Soissons, *Clovis* entered into negotiations with St. Remi, who, at the age of 22, had been elected Bishop of Rheims in 459, and whose long episcopate of seventy-four years is probably unique in history. On Christmas Day, A.D. 496, St. Remi, who had arranged the marriage of Clovis with the Christian princess Clotilde, baptized the Frankish king with his own hands in the Cathedral. This important event took place undoubtedly at Rheims and not at Tours, as a learned German, *Krusch*, has attempted to prove.

Under the Merovingians and Carolingians, the history of Rheims became merged in that of the French monarchy. The possession of the city was disputed as fiercely as that of the throne. The city was mixed up in quarrels from which it suffered, without, however, losing its religious prestige. Pépin-le-Bref and Pope Stephen III., Charlemagne and Pope Leo III. had famous interviews there. When the Carolingians restored the religious hierarchy Rheims became one of the twenty-two chief cities of the Empire. From the time of Charlemagne, the Archbishop of Rheims ruled over twelve bishoprics, comprising the cities of the ancient Roman province of *Belgica Secunda*.

From the 9th to the 11th century the history of Rheims is that of its church. The Counts of Vermandois, the Lords of Coucy and the archbishops first disputed, then divided its temporal possession, the latter falling eventually to the archbishops in the 11th century. After becoming Counts, with the right to coin money, and, from 940, powerful temporal princes, the archbishops played a great political part in the struggles between the Carolingian princes. Under *Charles-le-Chauve*, Archbishop Hincmar became the protector of the enfeebled monarchy. In 858 he prevented *Louis-le-Germanique* from deposing his nephew and becoming King of France. In 987, Archbishop Adalbéron, at the Meeting of Senlis, drove the legitimate heir, *Charles de Lorraine*, from the throne, and favoured the election of Hughes Capet. Although, under the Capetians, Paris became the political capital of France, Rheims became the religious metropolis of the kingdom. From the time when *Louis-le-Pieux* had himself consecrated emperor in the Cathedral, by Pope Stephen IV., it was understood that every new king must be consecrated by the successor of St. Remi.

The Consecration of the Kings of France

In the 12th century, Popes and Kings formally acknowledged the right of the Archbishop of Rheims to consecrate and crown the kings of France. As a matter of fact, until the Revolution, all the kings, except Louis IV. and Henri IV., were consecrated at Rheims.

The ceremony of consecration filled the Cathedral with a great crowd of people. Apart from the peers, numerous prelates, dignitaries of the Kingdom, the Court, the Chapter of the Cathedral and the populace crowded in. Staging was erected for the public in the transept ends and along the choir. Before the consecration took place, the archbishop, at the head of a procession, went to receive the *Sacred Ampulla* at the threshold of the Cathedral, brought on horseback by the Abbot of St. Remi. Returning to the altar, the prelate received the King's oath and then consecrated him, anointing him with the holy oil on his head and breast, between and on his shoulders, on the joints of his arms and in the palms of his hands, each motion being accompanied with a special prayer. Then the Peers handed the insignia of royalty to the archbishop, who, surrounded by all the Peers, placed the crown of Charlemagne on the head of the King, *while the people shouted* "*Long live the King.*"

The King was then led to a throne prepared for him at the entrance to the Choir, and mass was celebrated with great pomp. The King and Queen communicated in both kinds, and the royal party then went in procession to the archbishop's palace, where the *Feast of Consecration* was held.

In 1162, the Archbishopric of Rheims, until then a county, became a Duchy and the highest peerage in France, which explains why it was given to great personages, such as Henri-de-France and Guillaume-de-Champagne, brother and brother-in-law of Louis VII.

In the 12th century the archbishops, freed from the feudal rivalries, were confronted by a new power, the *bourgeoisie* or middle classes, born of the progress of industry and commerce, and whose importance was demonstrated by the great Champagne Fairs held sometimes at Rheims and sometimes at Troyes. The first *Company of Burgesses*, founded in 1138, soon became a "*Commune.*" In 1147, the suburb of St. Remi, which the archbishop refused to allow to become attached to the "*Commune,*" rose in revolt and was only appeased by the intervention of St. Bernard and Suger.

In 1160, Archbishop Henri-de-France, with the help of the Count of Flanders, who was occupying Rheims with a thousand horsemen, suppressed the "*Commune,*" whose independence was alarming him. In 1182 a royal charter, granting to the inhabitants the right to elect for a year twelve "*échevins*" (aldermen), re-established the *Commune* in fact, if not in name, but the struggle between the *Commune* and the archbishop still went on. In 1211, Philippe-Auguste compelled the aldermen to hand over the keys of the city gates to the archbishop.

In 1228, Archbishop Henri-de-Braine, not feeling himself safe in the city, built the fortified castle of Mars-Gate (or old castle of the archbishops) outside the walls, but looking towards the city (*photo, p.* 6). During the serious riots of 1235, the burgesses besieged the archbishop's castle, for which

THE CONSECRATION CEREMONY OF THE KINGS OF FRANCE IN THE CATHEDRAL OF RHEIMS (*see p.* 4)

act they were excommunicated by Pope Gregory IX., and rebuked by St. Louis. In 1257, St. Louis intervened once more, to put an end to the fighting between the free Companies of the Burghers and the soldiers of the archbishop.

In the 14th century the two adversaries frequently came to blows, until the king, in 1362, put an end to their quarrels by taking into his own hands the care and military government of Rheims.

In spite of these local struggles the city developed in the course of the Middle Ages. With Chartres it had a well-attended episcopal school, long before Paris. Among the masters of this school were *Gerbert,* one of the most learned men of the Middle Ages, who became Pope under the name of Sylvester II., and *St. Bruno,* founder of the Carthusian Order. Among the pupils were *Fulbert* (afterwards Bishop of Chartres), the historian *Richer, Guillaume de Champeaux,* and *Abélard* (adversary of St. Bernard).

During the Hundred Years' War (*see military section*) the Town Council of Rheims, which the Treaty of Troyes in 1420 had placed under the domination of the English, declared in favour of Charles VII., in spite of the Duke of Burgundy, who was residing at Laon, and notwithstanding the intrigues of the Bishop of Beauvais, Pierre Cauchon, who, profiting by the absence of the archbishop, went so far as to have a *Corpus Christi* procession in the city, to call down the blessing of Heaven upon the English. On July 17th, 1429, Joan-of-Arc handed over the keys of the city to the king, and was present at the consecration, standing near the altar with her standard which, "after having been through much tribulation, was accounted worthy of a place of honour." Since the return of Charles VII. to Rheims, the city had never ceased to be French. After the departure of the king and Joan-of-Arc, a friend of Pierre Cauchon plotted to deliver the town into the hands of the Duke of Burgundy, to whom the English promised it, provided he could take it. The plot was discovered and failed.

Under Louis XI. a serious revolt, known as the Micquemaque, broke out in the town. Louis, well received at the time of his consecration, had promised the people of Rheims (or so they believed) the abolition of the tax known as the "*taille.*" When, therefore, in the following year, the collectors demanded payment, the people rose in revolt and drove them out.

THE OLD CASTLE OF THE ARCHBISHOPS OF RHEIMS,
RAZED TO THE GROUND BY HENRI IV.

The Archbishops of Rheims were formerly powerful temporal lords (*see page* 4).

As usual, the king had recourse to treachery. Disguised as peasants, his soldiers entered the city unperceived. Once inside, they arrested those who were most deeply compromised, and carried out violent reprisals. Houses were plundered, many of the inhabitants banished, and nine put to death.

During the War of Religion, Rheims sided with the Catholics.

Under the influence of the *Guises*, five of whom were archbishops of Rheims (notably Cardinal Charles de Lorraine, the protector of Rabelais and Ronsard, and founder of the University of Rheims in 1547), the town espoused the cause of the League and opened its gates to the Duc de Mayenne in 1585. It submitted to Henri IV. only after the battle of Ivry, when the Castle of Mars Gate (stronghold of the archbishops) was razed to the ground. Henceforth the archbishops played no political part, and Richelieu put an end to strife by turning the *Guises* out of the archi-episcopal see.

In the 17th and 18th centuries the town lived in peace, with alternations of misery and suffering (caused by plague or famine) and commercial and industrial prosperity. It was at Rheims that the first French newspaper, the " Gazette de France," printed by Godard in 1694, appeared.

During the Revolution, Rheims received the new ideas with enthusiasm. It furnished a great number of volunteers to withstand the invasion, and on August 14th, 1792, the Legislative Assembly proclaimed that the city " *had deserved well of the country.*"

Under the Restoration its industry developed. In August, 1830, the people, who were favourably to the Revolution of July, overturned the cross of the " *Calvaire de la Mission,*" erected in 1821 by the ultra-Catholic party, and in its place set up a funeral urn with the inscription, " To the brave men who died for liberty on the 27th, 28th and 29th days of July, 1830." The population accepted the monarchy of July, but without enthusiasm.

The Second Empire witnessed a remarkable development of business activity which, after the momentary stoppage caused by the War of 1870 and the Prussian occupation (*see military section*), made of Rheims, at the end of the 19th century, one of the great commercial and industrial cities of France. The population increased from about 30,000 (in 1792) to 59,000 (in 1865) and to more than 115,000 in 1912.

When the War of 1914 broke out, the rich and ancient city was still as *La Fontaine* had described it :

" *No town is dearer to me than Rheims,*
The Honour and Glory of our France."

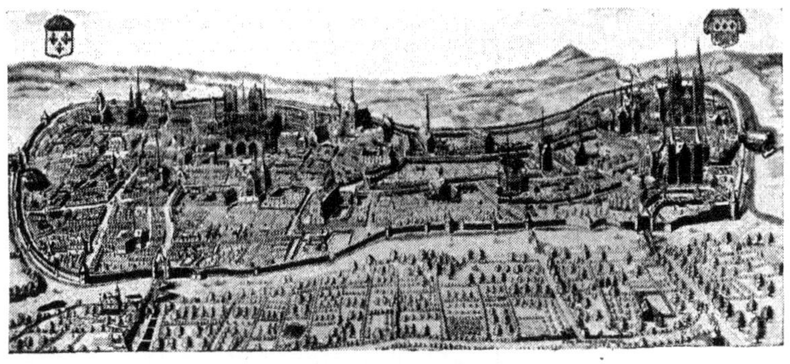

RHEIMS, FROM AN OLD ENGRAVING (1622)

MILITARY HISTORY

If the military and commercial situation of Rheims destined it, from early times, to be a great city, it also exposed it to the greed of ambitious foreigners, and opened the road to invasion.

During the Hundred Years' War the city was fiercely disputed. On December 4th, 1359, Edward III. of England besieged it. On January 11th, 1360, a sortie of the troops and burghers, under Remi Grammaire, compelled him to raise the siege, in recognition of which feat of arms Charles V. permitted the "*fleur-de-lys*" (emblem of the Royal House of France) to be emblazoned on the City's coat of arms. Since then the Shield of Rheims has been: In chief France ancient, in base argent Two, laurel branches in Saltire vert. In 1420 the English were more successful and entered Rheims, whose gates were opened to them by Philippe-le-Bon, Duke of Burgundy. Nine years later (July 16th, 1429) the Dauphin of France and Joan-of-Arc entered the town, then finally delivered, by the Dieu-Lumière Gate (formerly the Gate of St. Nicaise).

During the invasion of 1814, Marshal Marmont's troops retook Rheims on March 13th, after sharp street fighting, and Napoleon entered the city the same night.

In 1870, after the investment of Metz, Rheims witnessed the departure of the army formed by MacMahon at Châlons-sur-Marne, for the relief of Marshal Bazaine. A few days later (September 4th) the Prussian troops entered the city at 3 o'clock in the afternoon by three different gates. On the 6th, the King of Prussia, accompanied by Bismarck and Von Moltke, made an imposing entry, and resided for some time at the archi-episcopal palace, in the apartments reserved for the Kings of France at the time of their consecration. Rheims was held to ransom, and a number of citizens shot for protesting against the German yoke, chief among whom was the Abbé Miroy, Curé of Cuchery, whose tomb (the work of the sculptor Saint Marceaux) is in the northern cemetery. Others were carried away prisoners to Germany. The Prussian troops evacuated the town on November 20th, 1872.

The Invasion of 1914

(*See map, p.* 11.)

Forty-four years later to a day (September 4, 1914), German advance troops again entered Rheims, as General Joffre's plans had not provided for defending the city. However, the Army detachments placed under the command of General Foch on August 29, and wedged in between the 4th and 5th Armies, stayed the German advance for a few days. On August 30 the 42nd Division from the East, detrained at Rheims and took up positions at Sault-Saint-Rémy and Saint-Loup-en-Champagne on August 31, to the left of the 9th and 11th Corps.

On September 1, General Foch resisted on the river Retourne but, in the evening, withdrew to the river Suippe, in conformity with the general orders. On the 2nd the town was still protected by the 10th Corps (elements of which occupied the Fort of St. Thierry), by the 42nd Division near Brimont and to the north of the Aviation ground, and by the 9th and 11th Corps to the east. On the 3rd, the French retreat towards the Marne became more rapid, and Rheims was abandoned. On September 5, Prince August Wilhelm of Prussia entered the town and took up his quarters at the Grand Hôtel. The Germans at once requisitioned 50 tons of meat, 20 tons of vegetables, 100 tons of bread, 50 tons of oats, 15,000 gallons of petrol, besides straw and hay, and insisted on the immediate payment of a million francs as a guarantee that their requirements would be met.

THE TEMPORARY GERMAN OCCUPATION OF SEPT. 1914

German troops in front of the Cathedral. The scaffolding of the latter was set on fire on Sept. 19.

This sum was paid in the course of the afternoon, under threats by the enemy. From the 6th onwards the German soldiers gave themselves up to plundering. The tobacco warehouse at 21 Rue Payen was ransacked, and more than 700,000 francs worth of cigars and tobacco stolen. On the following days pillaging, especially of the food-shops, continued. On the 9th, the Kommandantur requisitioned civilians to bury the dead in the Rethel, Epernay and Montmirail districts. On the 11th, the Crown Prince arrived and took up his quarters at the Grand Hôtel, where he was joined by Prince Henry of Prussia, brother of the Kaiser. On the morning of the 12th, the Germans, alarmed at the approach of the victorious French troops from the Marne, arrested the Mayor (Dr. Langlet), Mgr. Neveux, coadjutor of Rheims, and the Abbé Camus. They then drew up a list of a hundred hostages and threatened to hang them at the first attempt at disorder. They also threatened to burn the city, wholly or partially, and to hang the inhabitants, if any of them molested the German soldiers. All that day the Germans, instead of organising defences, left the town in haste, after first pillaging it. In the afternoon the Crown Prince left the Grand Hôtel with his suite. At 5 p.m., after setting fire to the forage stores, the Kommandantur left Rheims by the Rethel road in drenching rain, followed by the hundred hostages, who were only released at the level-crossing at Witry-les-Rheims. When the latter returned to Rheims, a patrol of French mounted Chasseurs had already entered the town by the suburb of St. Anne. The next morning, at about 6 o'clock, the French troops, with the 6th mounted Chasseurs at their head, entered Rheims by the Rue de Vesle. At 1 p.m. General Franchet d'Espérey, commanding the French 5th Army, entered the city.

The Battles for Rheims, 1914-1918

Although evacuated by the Germans, Rheims had yet to remain for nearly four years under enemy fire. With equal obstinacy the adversaries disputed the town, the French seeking to disengage it and the Germans to recapture it.

On September 12, on the approach of the victorious French Army from the Marne, the Germans entrenched themselves to the south-west of the town, and established a line of resistance passing through Thillois, Ormes, Bezannes and Villers-aux-Noeuds.

In spite of the very unfavourable weather, the 3rd Corps (Gen. Hache) vigorously engaged the enemy at Thillois, and forced them to abandon the position in the evening. The 1st Corps (Gen. Deligny), on the right, had orders to push forward advance-guards into Rheims, but as a matter of fact they reached the suburb of Vesle. The 10th Corps (Gen. Defforges) attacked at Puisieulx and forced the enemy across the Vesle.

On the 13th, the left of the 3rd Corps arrived in front of Courcy and Brimont, where the Germans were strongly entrenched. A desperate battle took place, with the result that Courcy was taken before noon. Loivre likewise fell into the hands of the French, but the passage of the Aisne Canal was fiercely disputed. The attack on Brimont failed, in spite of the great valour of the troops, who sustained heavy losses. Meanwhile, the 1st Corps crossed Rheims, with orders to debouch at Bétheny. Just outside the town they were met with violent artillery fire, which, however, did not completely check their advance. La Neuvillette, Pierquin Farm and Bétheny were occupied, and the 1st Corps linked up on its left with the 3rd Corps, on the outskirts of Soulain Woods. The advance continued during the night, and Modelin Farm was reached by advance-guards. General Deligny took up his headquarters in the suburb of Vesle. The 10th Corps crossed the Vesle, engaged the enemy at St. Léonard and reached the railway.

On the 14th, the fighting greatly increased in violence. The 3rd Corps, in spite of repeated efforts, was unable to advance; on the left it failed to drive the enemy from the St. Marie Farm, while on the right it was held up before Brimont. The 1st Corps was likewise checked; the 1st Division (Gen. Gallet) attempted unsuccessfully to support General Hache in his attack on Brimont. The 10th Corps, although strongly engaged towards the Fort of La Pompelle, made but little progress. Farther away, on the right, the battle extended along the front of the 9th Army.

On the 15th, at 5.30 a.m., the 5th Army resumed a general offensive. Fierce fighting took place at St. Marie Farm, to the left of the 3rd Corps, and also further north, near Hill 100. Despite heavy sacrifices, however, the enemy held their positions; but, on the right, the 36th Infantry Regiment captured the Château of Brimont at day-break. General Deligny, less fortunate, was driven out of Soulains Woods, but stood firm at the Champ-de-Courses and Bétheny. The 10th Corps continued to advance slowly, and at certain points reached the high-road to Suippes.

On the 16th, the 3rd Corps attacked Brimont again, but failed. At the château the situation became more and more critical, by reason of the retreat of the 1st Corps on the previous day. This Corps had again to face a powerful enemy counter-offensive, which, however, failed to drive it from the Modelin Farm and the "Cavaliers de Courcy."

On the 17th, the Germans counter-attacked all along the line. In the afternoon the 3rd Corps, which stood firm at Godat Farm and Loivre, was elsewhere compelled to cross to the west bank of the canal and fall back on Courcy.

After a heroic defence the isolated garrison of Brimont Castle, weakened by heavy losses, surrendered during the night, after having spent all its ammunition. The 1st Corps, the greater part of which had left for the region of Berry-au-Bac, held its positions with its last available units. The 10th Corps extended its front westwards to Bétheny, while one of its regiments, the 2nd Infantry, occupied La Pompelle Fort.

On the 18th, the enemy increased their effrots against the front held by the 3rd Corps and the reserve units further west. Loivre, which had so far resisted, fell. The French withdrew to the west of the road to Laon. The situation was considered critical at this point of the front. The 10th Corps, which had been withdrawn from the east of Rheims, in favour of another sector, was stopped on the way and sent for a few days in support of the 3rd Corps.

On the 19th, one of its brigades counter-attacked Courcy Mill. On the other side, the Moroccan Division (Gen. Humbert), which had relieved the 10th Corps, continued to hold La Pompelle Fort.

Gradually the front became fixed. Desperate, indecisive fighting still took place, but finally the front stabilised on the line extending from the foot of the Berru and Nogent-l'Abbesse Hills, along the road from Rheims to Suippes, on the east, and along the western bank of the Aisne Canal on the north.

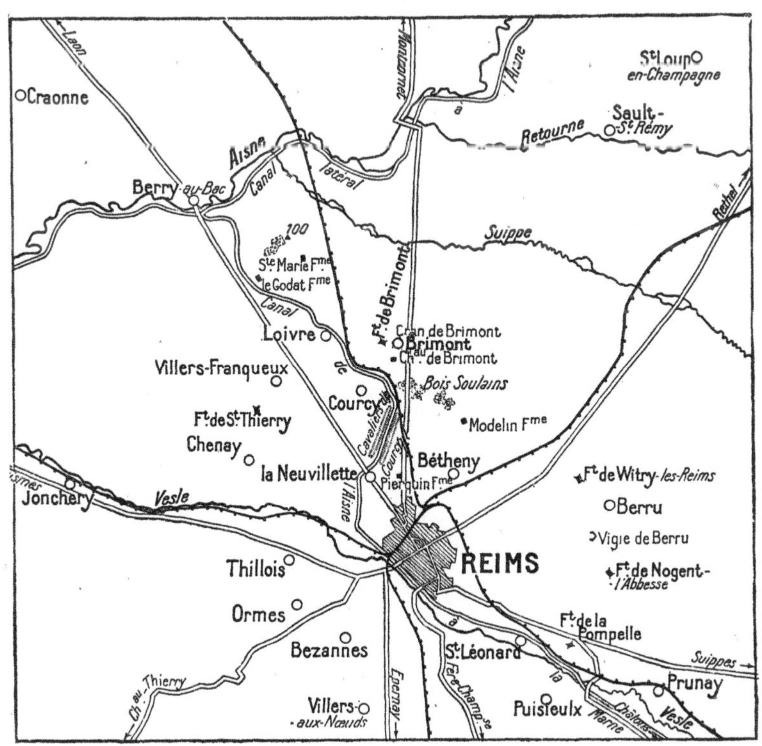

EXPLANATORY MAP OF THE MILITARY OPERATIONS IN 1914

(*See pp.* 9-11.)

The French Offensive of April, 1917

The French offensive, planned by the then Commander-in-Chief, General Nivelle, and launched in April, between Soissons and Auberive, aimed at piercing the German front and disengaging Rheims.

North-west of Rheims was the 5th Army (Gen. Mazel), of which the 38th Corps (Gen. de Mondesir) held the immediate approaches to the town, followed by the 7th Corps (Gen. de Bazelaire), 32nd Corps (Gen. Passaga) astride the Aisne, and, extending beyond Craonne, the 5th Corps (Gen. de Boissoudy) and the 1st Corps (Gen. Muteau).

East of Rheims the 4th Army (Gen. Anthoine) was engaged only during the second stage of the battle.

At 6 a.m. on the 16th, in drenching rain, the 5th Army attacked all along the front, in conjunction on the left with the 6th Army (Gen. Mangin), which undertook to storm the Chemin-des-Dames. The enemy was expecting the attack, and had concentrated very large forces and powerful artillery. Despite their bravery, the French were unable to break through.

In the Rheims sector, the 32nd Corps advanced three kilometers to the

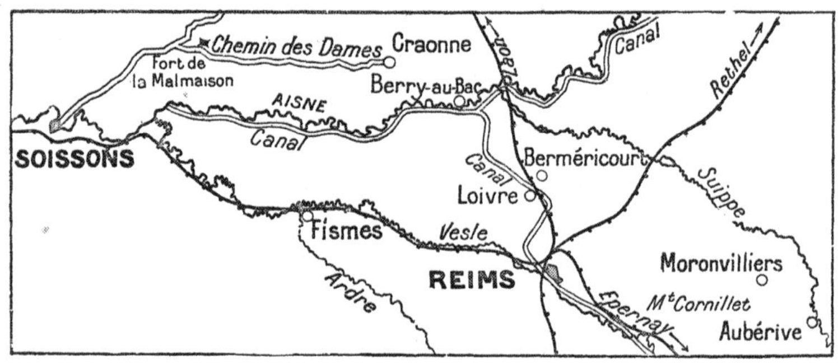

EXPLANATORY MAP OF THE MILITARY OPERATIONS IN 1917

north of the Aisne. The 7th Corps crossed the canal at Loivre and captured Berméricourt in the morning, but was forced to give up part of the conquered ground in the afternoon, in consequence of a powerful German counter-attack. In front of Brimont a brigade of the 38th Corps failed to pierce the enemy's positions.

On the 17th, while the army of General Mazel resisted a violent enemy counter-atack, General Anthoine attacked from the east of Rheims to Auberive with the 8th Corps (Gen. Hély d'Oissel), 17th Corps (Gen. J. B. Dumas), 12th Corps (Gen. Nourrisson). At 4.45 a.m., despite violent squalls of rain and snow, the French infantry rushed forward and carried the first German lines along a front of eleven kilometers. The 34th Division (Gen. de Lobit) carried the Mont Cornillet and Mont Blond hills, which the enemy attempted in vain to recapture.

On April 18 and 19, and May 4 and 5, the fighting was spasmodic and finally ceased. On the whole, the French offensive failed, and Rheims continued to remain under enemy gun-fire.

On the morning of May 27, 1918, the Germans commenced a powerful offensive between Vauxaillon (on the Chemin-des-Dames) and the Fort of Brimont. At the beginning of the attack, the French line passed through Bétheny and along the Aisne-Marne Canal. In the evening, after the loss of the Chemin-des-Dames and the Aisne Canal, Rheims was no longer protected on the north-west, except by the St. Thierry Heights, which were soon turned. The Germans crossed the Vesle at several points, principally at Bazoches and Fismes, and advanced as far as Muizon.

On May 29, the French line passed through La Neuvillette, Châlons-sur-Vesle, Muizon and Rosnay. On the 30th, it extended from Perquin Farm to Méry-Premecy, via Champigny. On the 31st, Tinqueux and Vrigny fell.

Further to the south the Germans advanced along the valley of the Ardre towards the Château-Thierry—Epernay—Châlons railway, threatening Epernay (*see the Michelin Guide: "The Second Battle of the Marne"*).

However, Rheims still held out. On June 1, the Germans attacked simultaneously, without success, to the south-east of the town (between Pommery Park and La Pompelle Fort), and on the west and south-west (between La Haubette and Ormes), while the French recaptured Vrigny. On three seperate occasions—in the evening of the 1st, and on June 9 and 18, the enemy's powerful and costly efforts to recapture this important position broke down. On the 18th, they delivered a fresh general attack from Vrigny to La Pompelle, gaining a footing in the Northern Cemetery of Rheims and in the north-eastern outskirts of Sillery, but everywhere else they were repulsed. On the 23rd and 29th, they rushed Bligny Hill, held by the Italians, only to lose it again shortly afterwards. Once again, Rheims had eluded the enemy's grasp.

July 15 to August 9, 1918

At dawn, on July 15, the Germans began a new offensive from Château-Thierry to La Main de Massiges. It was Ludendorf's much vaunted "Friedensturm" (peace-battle), and was expected by him to prove irresistible and

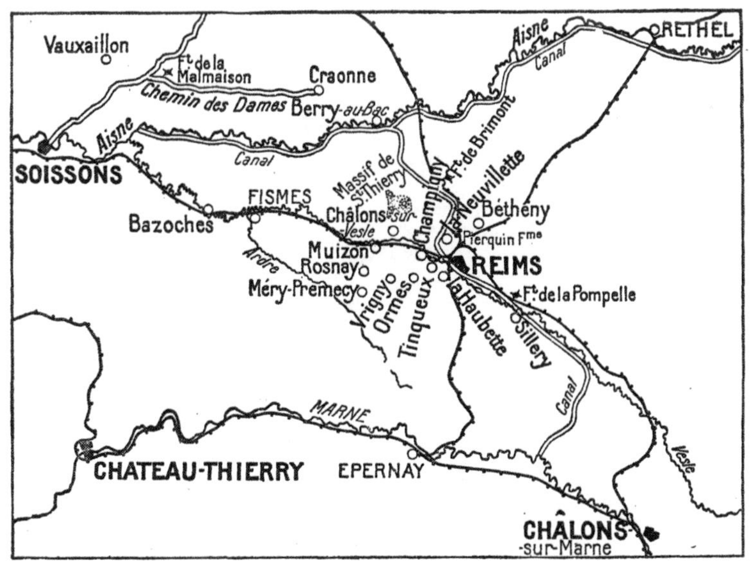

EXPLANATORY MAP OF THE MILITARY OPERATIONS DESCRIBED ABOVE

decisive. Its purpose was to complete the encirclement of Rheims, carry the hills surrounding the town, crush the French 4th Army, and reach Châlons-sur-Marne (*see the Michelin Guide : " Champagne and Argonne "*). However, this time, there was no surprise, and the Allies held out victoriously.

To the west, between Dormans and Rheims, Franco-Italian forces held their ground on the Châtillon-sur-Marne—Cuchery—Marfaux—Bouilly line. To the east, from La Pompelle to the Argonne, the army of General Gouraud, after voluntarily abandoning its first line previous to the enemy's attack, checked and decimated the armies of Von Einem and Von Mudra, on its second or battle-line. On July 16, 17 and 18, the enemy, now exhausted and incapable of resuming their general attack, attempted local attempts only, especially near Beaumont-sur-Vesle, to the north of Prosnes, and in the region of Trigny and Pourcy, to the west, all of which were repulsed. Once more Rheims escaped, and was destined from now on, to be gradually freed from the enemy's grasp. The French counter-offensive began on July 18, on the Aisne (*see the Michelin Guide : " The Second Battle of the Marne "*), extending shortly afterwards to the west of Rheims. On the 22nd, the army of General Berthelot captured St. Euphraise and Bouilly, and on the 23rd reached a point between Vrigny and the Ardre. A number of German counter-attacks on July 24, 25 and 30 and August 1 failed to check its advance. On August 2, Gueux and Thillois were recaptured. On the 4th, the Vesle was reached to the east of Fismes, and the latter occupied, while a small force crossed to the north bank of the river. On the 7th, after fierce fighting, in which the French and Americans advanced foot by foot, the Vesle was crossed to the east of Bazoches and Braine. On the 9th, Fismette was taken.

September 26 to November 11, 1918

The disengaging of Rheims, which had begun slowly, was now rapidly accomplished. Two French offensives completely effected it in a few days—

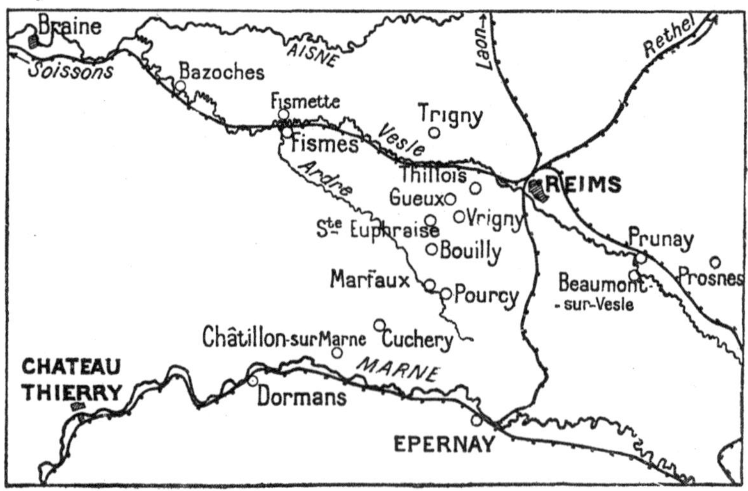

that of September 26 (*see the Michelin Guide: "Champagne and Argonne"*), under General Gouraud, and that of September 30, first by General Berthelot and then by General Guillaumat. The first of these offensives, to the east, brought about the fall of the Moronvilliers Heights, after outflanking them; the second, to the west, captured the Saint-Thierry Heights, the French troops crossing the Aisne-Marne Canal from Le Godat to La Neuvillette. This double manœuvre forced the Germans, whose communications were threatened, to beat a hasty retreat on October 5 along a twenty-seven mile front. An important part of the old German front of 1914, and one of the most fiercely disputed, collapsed suddenly. The formidable forts of Brimont and Nogent-l'Abbesse, which had held Rheims under their guns for four years, fell. This time the deliverance of Rheims was complete and final.

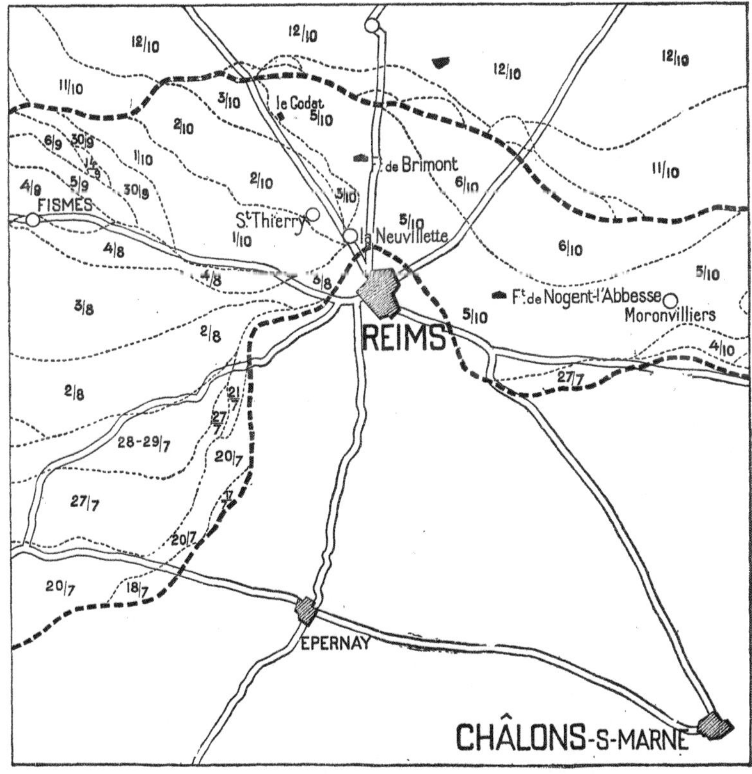

THE DISENGAGING OF RHEIMS

The dotted lines show the Allied advance at the date indicated in the middle of each zone conquered. The line of departure is that of July 18 (18/7). On the evening of Oct. 6 (6/10)—the upper thick dotted line—the town was completely disengaged. The Allied advance has the appearance of a fan spreading out west of Rheims until Oct. 5 (5/10), when the Germans were forced to make a deep retreat.

The Destruction of Rheims

Being unable to capture Rheims, the Germans reduced it to ruins by bombardment. For four years (September 4, 1914, to October 5, 1918) they rained explosive and incendiary shells on it, almost without intermission.

On September 3, 1914, at about 11 a.m., a German aeroplane dropped bombs on the town. A few of the inhabitants left, as the enemy approached, but the majority remained. A lady-teacher, sixty years of age, Mlle. Fouriaux (afterwards decorated with the Legion d'Honneur), who had charge of Hospital No. 101 (formerly a high-school for girls), transferred the wounded to Epernay and then returned on foot to Rheims.

On September 4, at 9.30 a.m., when the enemy advance-guards were already in the town, and a German officer was making requisitions at the Town Hall, the bombardment began again. From 9.30 to 10.15 a.m., 176 large shells fell into the town, three of which tore open the great gallery of modern paintings in the Museum. Forty-nine civilians were killed and 130 wounded, several of them mortally.

The Germans, hard pressed by the French, evacuated Rheims on September 12. Two days later, at 9 a.m., they bombarded the town. Their fire was especially directed against the headquarters of General Franchet d'Esperey, near the Town Hall. On the following days, firing was resumed at the same hour. On the 17th, the first fires broke out. Many civilians were killed or wounded. The vicinity of the Cathedral, which was believed to be specially aimed at, was among the places that suffered most. To protect the Cathedral, which the Germans had fitted up on the 12th for the reception of their wounded, some seventy to eighty German wounded were accommodated on straw in the nave. The Red Cross flag was displayed on each tower, and notice given to the enemy.

GERMAN SHELLS BURSTING IN A STREET OF RHEIMS

THE MONT DE PIÉTÉ

On the 18th, the bombardment began again at 8.15 a.m. In addition to the Sub-Prefecture, which was almost entirely destroyed, as were also many important factories, the Cathedral, in spite of the Red Cross flag, was struck by 8-in. shells, which damaged the outside sculptures of the lower windows of the main transept, smashing the 13th and 14th century stained-glass. Splinters of stone killed a French gendarme and two wounded Germans in the lower part of the south nave.

On the 19th, the bombardment was intensified. The Town Hall, Museum, hospitals (including that of the Girls' High School), the south side of the Cathedral and the Archbishop's Palace were all hit. Towards noon, incendiary shells were rained on the centre of the town.

At about 4 p.m., a shell fired the wooden scaffolding round the north-west tower which had been under repair since 1913. The fire spread quickly to the roof, the molten lead from which set fire to the straw in the nave.

THE SAINT FRÈRES FACTORY IN RUINS (OCT. 1916)
(15 *Rue de l'University*)

CENTRAL WOOL CONTROL OFFICE IN SEPT., 1915

In spite of a rescue party, who risked their lives in getting out the wounded, a dozen of the German wounded perished in the flames. The conflagration spread to the Archbishop's Palace, from which it was impossible to remove the tapestries or the prehistoric Roman and Gothic collections. The Protestant Church, the Offices of the Controller of silk and woollen cloths, and the Colbert barracks along the eastern boulevards were burnt. Everywhere new centres caught fire, and nearly thirty-five acres of buildings were destroyed. On the 20th, the bombardment continued with equal violence, then after a respite of two days began again. Of the Place Royale and the Rue Colbert nothing remained but a heap of ruins.

THE PROTESTANT CHURCH IN AUGUST, 1917

(Boulevard Lundy)

KINDERGARTEN SCHOOL IN THE BOULEVARD LUNDY

On November 1 the number of civilians killed by shell fire had increased to 282.

From September 14, 1914, to the beginning of June, 1915, the town never remained more than four days without being shelled. Up to the end of November, 1914, the shells rarely went beyond the Cathedral and the theatre, falling mostly in the suburbs of Cérès and Laon. On November 22, the suburb of Paris was struck, and from that time onwards there was no security for the inhabitants in any quarter of the city.

As it would take too long to recount all the bombardments, only the most terrible ones are here mentioned. On November 26, 1914, the German guns fired all day, one shell alone killing twenty-three patients in the Hospital for Incurables. On the night of February 21 and on February 22, 1915, more than 1,500 shells fell in the town, killing twenty civilians, setting on fire a score of houses and piercing the vaulting of the Cathedral.

RUE GAMBETTA

The Cathedral is seen at the end of the street.

On March 8, terrifying fires broke out again. On April 29 and July 20 more than 500 shells, many of them incendiary, were counted. In April, 1916, more than 1,200 projectiles struck the different quarters of the town in one day. On August 13, whilst the town was being bombarded, seven German aeroplanes dropped incendiary bombs, which burnt the Hôtel Dieu Hospital. On October 25, the Germans fired more than 600 shells into Rheims and more than 1,000 on the 27th.

On April 1, 1917, more than 2,800 shells fell in the town, and on the 4th, 2,121. According to the Official Communiqué, on the night of the 5th and on Good Friday, the number of shells was 7,500. Easter-Day was likewise terrible. On April 15, 19 and 24 the town received large numbers of

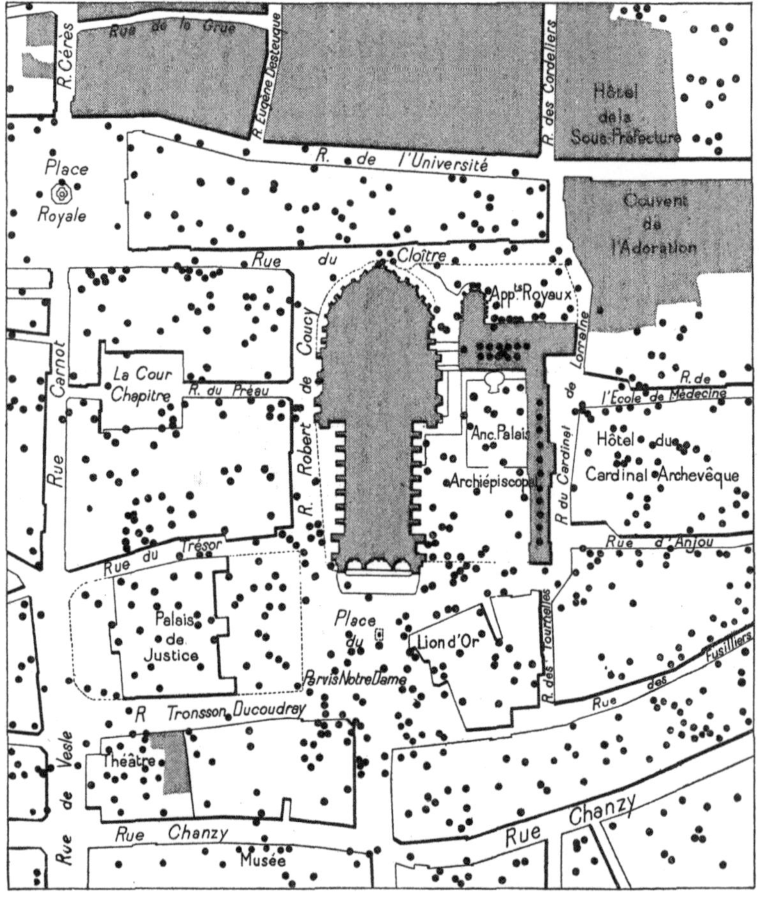

THE BOMBARDMENT OF THE CATHEDRAL QUARTER

Part of the striking-points of the shells which fell around the Cathedral, as noted by the architect of the latter (M. Sainsaulieu). The shells which struck the Cathedral were far too numerous to allow all of them to be shown on the above plan

8-in., 12-in. and 15-in. shells. On May 3 the Town Hall and 108 houses were burnt. On the 4th the fires spread to fifteen neighbouring streets.

From April 8 to the 15th the enemy rained incendiary shells on the town without respite, and completed their work of destruction, in the course of the afternoon of the 21st, by burning the centre of the town. Hardly anybody was left in the latter, except the firemen, who, despite their prodigious activity and valour, were unable to cope with the flames.

Whole streets, often the finest, were burnt down, more than 700 houses being destroyed.

When, on October 5, the Germans retreated, the havoc caused by this continual bombardment was incalculable. Of the town's 14,000 houses, only about sixty were immediately habitable when the people came back.

In addition to the material losses, there were, unfortunately, numerous irreparable artistic and archæological losses.

Life in Bombarded Rheims

Although there were short respites, it may be said that for four years Rheims led the life of a besieged town, under the fire of the German guns and howitzers. The enemy increased the calibre of their shells and varied their modes of bombardment, sometimes firing for a few hours, sometimes all day

THE DESTRUCTIONS, PHOTOGRAPHED FROM AN AEROPLANE *(Cliché Illustration)*

ND.—The Cathedral.
PR.—Place Royale.
D.—Hôtel de la Douane.
SG.—Société Générale Bank.
P.—General Post Office.
J.—Palais de Justice.
T.—Theatre.
M.—Museum.
GH.—Grand Hôtel.
LO.—Hôtel du Lion d'Or.
PA.—Archi-episcopal Palace.
A.—The Cardinal's House.
EP.—Professional School for Young Ladies.
SP.—Sub-Prefecture.
PG.—Place Godinot.
L.—Lycée.
C.—Colbert Barracks.

THE FIRST AND SECOND STORIES OF A HOUSE IN THE RUE D'ANJOU, AFTER THE BURSTING OF AN 8-IN. SHELL

long at the rate of one shell every three minutes, or again at night. Sometimes 3-in. shells would be used, at others "Jack Johnsons" of 8-in., 12-in. and 15-in. calibre; sometimes all four at the same time. Both explosive and incendiary shells were used, while aeroplane bombs, darts and asphyxiating gas were resorted to occasionally. Public holidays were the occasion of the fiercest bombardments, in the hope of increasing the number of victims. For instance, the shelling was particularly murderous on All Saints' Day of 1914, when the eastern and southern cemeteries (generally crowded on this day) were especially aimed at. Easter Monday of 1916 and Good Friday of 1917 were similarly favoured.

After each check—at Verdun, in Champagne, on the Somme or wherever it might be—the Germans revenged themselves on Rheims. In this way the Cathedral was fired by incendiary shells after the defeat on the Marne in 1914. The awful fires of February 22 and March 8, 1915, were the German reply to their set-backs in Champagne and Argonne. The Hôtel Dieu hospital was burnt down in August, 1916, the day after the Franco-British attack on the Somme. The Town Hall was reduced to ashes on May 3, 1917, after the French offensive on the Champagne hills. For the same reason the bombardments reached their maximum of intensity in April and May, 1918, *i.e.* after the enemy had lost all hope of crushing the Allies and taking Paris.

THE EFFECT OF AN 8-IN. SHELL IN THE PREMISES OF "LA MUTUALITÉ," IN THE RUE DES ELUS (SEPT. 8, 1915)

At the beginning of the siege the population took refuge in the south-western districts, which were not as yet bombarded, but on and after November 22, 1914, when the German shells reached the suburb of Paris, a large number of the inhabitants left the town.

In February, 1915, the exodus began again, but at the end of May in that year there were still some 26,000 people in the town. In February, 1917, after twenty-eight months of bombardment, there remained 17,100 people, or 100,000 fewer than in 1914. At the beginning of April in that year, the mayor and later the sub-prefect, requested all those who were not prevented by their duties to leave the town.

This invitation not having the desired effect, the military authorities, in view of the increased intensity of the bombardment and the imminence of the French offensive, announced that they could not guarantee food supplies for the town, and decided that the civil population must leave not later than April 10. The evacuation was effected by carts and motor-vehicles to Epernay, where trains awaited the people.

A part of the inhabitants returned to Rheims after the French offensive of April–May, but for a few months only, as, in February, 1918, the coming German offensive compelled the civil population again to leave the town.

During the thirty-one months, during which a considerable portion of the population persisted in staying in Rheims (September, 1914, to April, 1917), life and work went on in the bombarded city, the people adapting themselves courageously to their precarious existence and to the danger. They were supplied with helmet and gas masks, like the soldiers. Shell and bomb-proof shelters were organised, and the cellars, with which the city abounds, became the people's ordinary dwellings. The Town Council, with the exception of a few members who left on the approach of the enemy, remained at the Town Hall until it was destroyed, then installed themselves in a cellar, under the constant chairmanship of the Mayor, Dr. Langlet. The services rendered by the latter during these trying times were such that the French Premier decorated him personally in November, 1914, with the *Croix de la Légion d'Honneur*. The General Post Office had to change its quarters several times; but until the complete evacuation of the town the postmen went their rounds regularly.

The Courts of Justice were set up in the cellars of the Palais-de-Justice.

The archbishop, Mgr. Luçon, was absent from Rheims in 1914, being retained in Rome by the Council. As soon as the latter was ended, he

REMOVING THE WORKS OF ART
IN JANUARY, 1918

SCHOOL CHILDREN WITH GAS-MASKS

returned to Rheims and thereafter, like his coadjutor, Mgr. Neveux, and the unmobilized clergy, he remained at his post until the evacuation of April, 1917. The Cathedral architect, M. Sainsaulieu, who, like Mgr. Luçon, has been made a Chevalier de la Légion d'Honneur, remained constantly at his post, repairing from day to day, as well as might be, the damage caused to the Cathedral, and saving the art treasures spared by the German shells.

The firemen, reinforced in March, 1915, by thirty two of their comrades from Paris, devoted themselves, at the risk of their lives, to fighting the flames caused by the bombardments. Unfortunately, their courage and devotion were often unequal to their task. For instance, twenty-two separate fires occurred on the night of February 22, 1915. Their task was rendered still more difficult by the fact that the Germans often fired on the burning buildings to drive off the men who were trying to save them.

On July 6, 1917, the President of the French Republic fittingly acknowledged the magnificent bravery of the firemen by personally decorating their flag with the Croix de la Légion d'Honneur. At the same time he conferred this dignity on the city (*see p.* 2).

After remaining closed for several weeks, the schools re-opened. Until then, the children had been too much in the streets looking for aluminium fuses of shells, out of which they made rings, or for scraps of stained-glass from the broken windows of the Cathedral. The first school, called the "Maunoury" school, was installed on December 7, 1914, in a wine cellar of the firm Pommery, Boulevard Henri-Vasnier, near the Rond-Point St. Nicaise. On January 22, 1915, the "Joffre" school was opened in the cellars of Messrs. Mumm, 24 Rue du Champ-de-Mars. Then came the "Albert I." school, in the cellars of Messrs. Krug, 5 Rue Coquebert, and the "Dubail" school in those of Messrs. Champion, Place St. Nicaise. In addition to the underground schools, open-air classes were conducted. The underground schools, in which the teaching staff, exclusively voluntary, lived permanently, together with the school-children and their relatives, were situated in the most exposed and frequently bombarded districts. The "Dubail" school was struck three times: on March 6, 1915 (by an 8-in. shell), and on March 25 and October 25, 1916. Luckily there were no victims.

The schools were quite close to the enemy lines, the distance varying from about two-thirds of a mile to a mile and a half.

In 1915 and 1916, the examinations for the "Elementary School Certificate" took place in July, as usual. In 1915, the ceremony of the Annual Prize Distribution, which had not taken place at Rheims for ten years, was restored, the book-prizes for the pupils coming from every corner of France.

The victualling of the town, thanks to the co-operation between the

CARDINAL LUÇON, ARCHBISHOP OF RHEIMS, COMING OUT OF THE CATHEDRAL

MILK-WOMAN, WITH HELMET, GOING HER ROUND

Municipal and Military Authorities, was effected with regularity. There was never any shortage of bread. The butchers' and grocers' shops remained open. The milk-women and hawkers donned their helmets and continued to push their carts through the streets. The market-women remained at their stalls. The nuns of St. Vincent-de-Paul, whose convent had been largely destroyed, ensured the service of cheap meals, organised by the Municipality for the poor. The undaunted inhabitants had their daily paper ("*L'Eclaireur de l'Est*"), edited by M. Dramas, a courageous journalist, whose printing-house was early wrecked by shell-fire, but who continued almost single-handed to issue his paper.

WINE-CELLAR OF MESSRS. POMMERY USED AS A DWELLING

PANORAMIC VIEW, SEEN FROM ST. NICAISE HILL (*p.* 102)

A VISIT TO RHEIMS

(*pp.* 28 *to* 120)

THE CATHEDRAL (*pp.* 28 *to* 60)

FIRST ITINERARY (*pp.* 61 *to* 94)

The Archi-episcopal Palace, Museum, Church of St. Jacques, Promenades, Town Hall, Place Royale, Musicians' House, Mars Gate, Faubourg Cérès, Church of St. André, Palais-de-Justice, etc.

SECOND ITINERARY (*pp.* 95 *to* 120

The Lycée, Abbey of St. Pierre-les-Dames, Rue Barbâtre, Church of St. Maurice, Church of St. Remi, Hôtel-Dieu Hospital, etc.

GERMAN PRISONERS CLEARING A STREET (OCT., 1918)

The Cathedral

The Cathedral of Rheims, which Charles VIII. declared to be "pre-eminent among all the churches of the kingdom," and which a local poet in the reign of Louis XIII. extolled above the seven wonders of the world, is one of the most beautiful Gothic churches extant.

Few edifices combine such grandeur, simplicity and grace ; still fewer, its characteristic unity and symmetry.

The work of at least four architects, the building operations extended over two centuries, yet it has retained rare unity both of plan and style. The whole is so harmonious as to give the impression of being the effort of a single master-mind.

Historical Account

The Cathedral stands on the site of former churches, successively erected between the 5th and 13th centuries. On the night of May 6, 1210, a terrible fire destroyed the then existing edifice, together with a portion of the city.

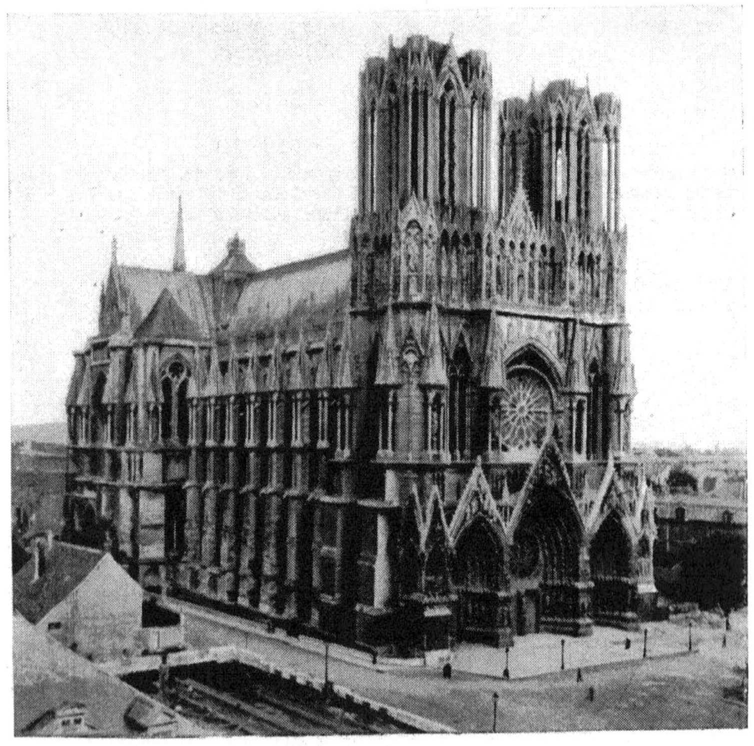

THE CATHEDRAL BEFORE THE WAR

Exactly one year later, Archbishop Aubri de Humbert laid the first stone of a new edifice, which was destined to become the Cathedral of to-day.

Begun in 1211, the building went on without pause for twenty years, after which there was a slackening, followed by a vigorous resumption in 1299. Another pause occurred during the Hundred Years' War. The Cathedral, less the tower spires provided for in the plans, was finished in 1428. The spires were not yet built when the great fire of July 24th, 1481, entirely destroyed the roof of the Cathedral, further deferring their construction, which was subsequently abandoned.

The funds for this colossal work were furnished partly by the clergy and the people, partly by Papal Indulgences granted to donors, and by collections in Christian lands, especially in the ecclesiastical province of Rheims. The wonderful plans of the Cathedral were long believed to be the work of *Robert de Coucy*, whereas the original ones were in fact drawn by *Jean d'Orbais*, who began their execution between 1211 and 1231. His work was continued with wonderful fidelity by *Jean-le-Loup*, from 1231–1247 ; by *Gaucher of Rheims* in 1247–1255, *Bernard of Soissons* from 1255 to 1290, *Robert de Coucy* until 1311, and afterwards by *Maître Çolard*, *Gilles le Maçon*, *Jean de Dijon* and *Colard de Givry* in the course of the 14th and 15th centuries.

THE CATHEDRAL AFTER THE FIRE OF SEPT. 19, 1914

In the 17th and 18th centuries only repairs rendered necessary by the wear of the stone were effected. In the 19th century, beginning in 1845, important restorations, principally by Viollet-le-Duc, were carried out with regularity.

The Cathedral's approximate measurements are 480 feet long (it is the longest church in France), and 160 feet wide at the intersection of the transept. The vaulting, less lofty than that at Beauvais (156 feet) and Amiens (143 feet), is 123 feet in height. The towers are six in number (as in the cathedral at Laon), of which the four situated at the extremities of the transept have never had more than one storey. The principal towers are about 266 feet in height, or about 60 feet higher than those of Notre-Dame in Paris.

The plan of the Cathedral is in shape a Latin cross, with radiating chapels. It is built entirely of stone from the neighbourhood of Rheims. Forty pillars support the vaults, which are further sustained by fifty buttresses. Three great doorways and eight secondary doors give access to the interior, which is lighted by a hundred windows and rose-windows; 2,303 figures of all sizes decorate the exterior and interior.

THE CATHEDRAL PHOTOGRAPHED FROM AEROPLANE IN 1916

The Cathedral During the War

In revenging themselves on Rheims for their disappointments and failures, the Germans seem to have been particularly determined to destroy the building which is at once one of the most precious artistic treasures of France and one of the most ancient evidences of her history. In 1814 the then Allies bombarded Rheims but respected the Cathedral. It is true that there were Germans who found fault with this respectful forbearance. One of them, *Johann Joseph Goëres,* author of a voluminous work entitled "*Christian Mysticism,*" dared to write in April, 1814: "*Destroy, reduce to ashes, this Rheims basilica, where Chlodovic was consecrated, and where was born that empire of the Franks, those turncoat brothers of the noble Germans; burn the Cathedral.*" In the course of the recent war the Germans followed the vindictive advice of Goëres, although, less frank than he, they did not dare, in face of the indignation of Christendom and of the whole world, boast of their vandalism.

By way of excuse they alleged sometimes errors in firing, sometimes that the French had established a battery of artillery near the Cathedral and an observation-post in one of the towers (a projector was installed on

THE PIERCED VAULTING AND TOWERS OF THE CATHEDRAL IN 1919

the Cathedral, on September 13, 1914, *i.e.* the day that the French re-entered Rheims, and it remained there only one night).

On November 9, 1914, General Rouquerol declared to the French Government, who had demanded an enquiry, that the nearest battery to the Cathedral was at that time more than 1,200 yards away ; that on the day (September 19) the Cathedral was set on fire by the German shells, the nearest French batteries were still quite close to the spot occupied by the above-mentioned battery, whose position the French Premier verified personally. The General concluded that the German artillery could not have made an error of 1,200 yards in firing, but that they had deliberately aimed at the Cathedral.

The Cathedral, though terribly shattered, is still standing. The description of the edifice (pp. 33 to 60) gives particulars of the damage and destructions which occurred principally in September, 1914, April, 1917, and July, 1918.

On September 19, 1914, incendiary shells set fire to various portions of the building. The roof was burnt, but the vaulting escaped injury. The tambours of the side doors and the statues on the latter were destroyed by the flames. The 18th century stalls, consecration carpet of Charles X. and archi-episcopal throne were likewise burnt. The great rose-window of the western façade, together with several other stained-glass windows, were destroyed, as were also the " Angel " steeple and its caryatids above the chevet. The northern tower was seriously injured by the burning of the scaffolding around it (*see photo, p.* 9). The statues were eaten into by the flames and subsequently crumbled away, some of them being irrecoverably lost.

In 1915 and 1916 the Cathedral was struck a hundred times, but it was during the bombardments of April 15, 19 and 24, 1917, that it suffered most. For seven consecutive hours, at the rate of twelve per hour, the Germans fired 12-in., 14-in. and 15-in. shells on the edifice, causing terrible havoc, especially to the south-western side.

During the terrible bombardments of April, 1918, the Cathedral did not suffer—for once the Germans seemed to have decided to spare it ; but, unfortunately, the truce did not last. In the following months the bombardment began again, and the ravages increased, especially in the two towers and the vaulting. However, both vaulting and towers, in spite of their injuries, have not been irreparably damaged in their vital parts, and are capable of restoration.

That the damage is not more serious is due to the protective measures taken by the Cathedral architect and by the Department of Historical Monuments. As early as 1915, the doorways of the western façade were protected with beams and sand-bags (*see photo, p.* 25), while the Treasure was removed and placed in safety, together with the paintings and tapestries.

In 1916 and following years masonry protections were placed around some of the more valuable statues. The fallen fragments of carvings and sculpture were carefully collected, with a view to future restoration. In this way the débris of the head of the beautiful statue of the " Visitation " Group, known as the " Smile of Rheims," on the left-hand side of the central doorway of the western façade, were saved.

At the beginning of 1918, it was found possible to save the remains of the stained-glass of the windows, and other glass-work still intact—amongst which was some of the finest in the nave. The salvage was difficult, for scaffolding would have furnished the Germans with an excuse for further bombardments. Recourse was had to a small body of Paris firemen and two glaziers who, in foggy weather, and before daybreak, climbed up to the iron frame-work of the windows and accomplished their work at great heights with remarkable courage and skill.

A
B
C
D
E
1
2
3
4
5
6
7
8
AÉRODROME MILITAIRE
LES TROIS FONTAINES
LE FOND PATÉ
R. Desbureaux
R. Danton
Bd Charles Arnould
R. de Magneux
Ernest Renan
FAUB. DE LAON
Bd Jules César
CIMETIÈRE DU NORD
Champ de Mars
R. Gosset
R. G. H. Mumm
FAUB. CÉRÈS
FAUB. DE CLAIRMARAIS
Av. de Brébant
R. du Bois d'Amour
GARE
PROMENADES
VESLE
Chemin de Tinqueux
R. de Tinqueux
Av. de Paris
FAUB. DE VESLE
R. Libergier
R. Chanzy
R. de Vesle
COMPIÈGNE 95
SOISSONS 53
Fismes 27
LA HAUBETTE
Vélodrome
PROVINS 111
MONTMIRAIL 67
CHATEAU-THIERRY 63
R. des Mesneux
CIMETIÈRE DE L'OUEST
R. de Bézannes
R. de Chamery
Courlancy
COURLANCY
Bd Fléchambault
Promenades
FAUBOURG
FLÉCHAMBAULT
CIMETIÈRE DU SUD
Chemin de Bézannes
LA MAISON BLANCHE
Route de Dormans
N. 51
TROYES 131
SENS 149
ÉPERNAY 27
Le Rouillat

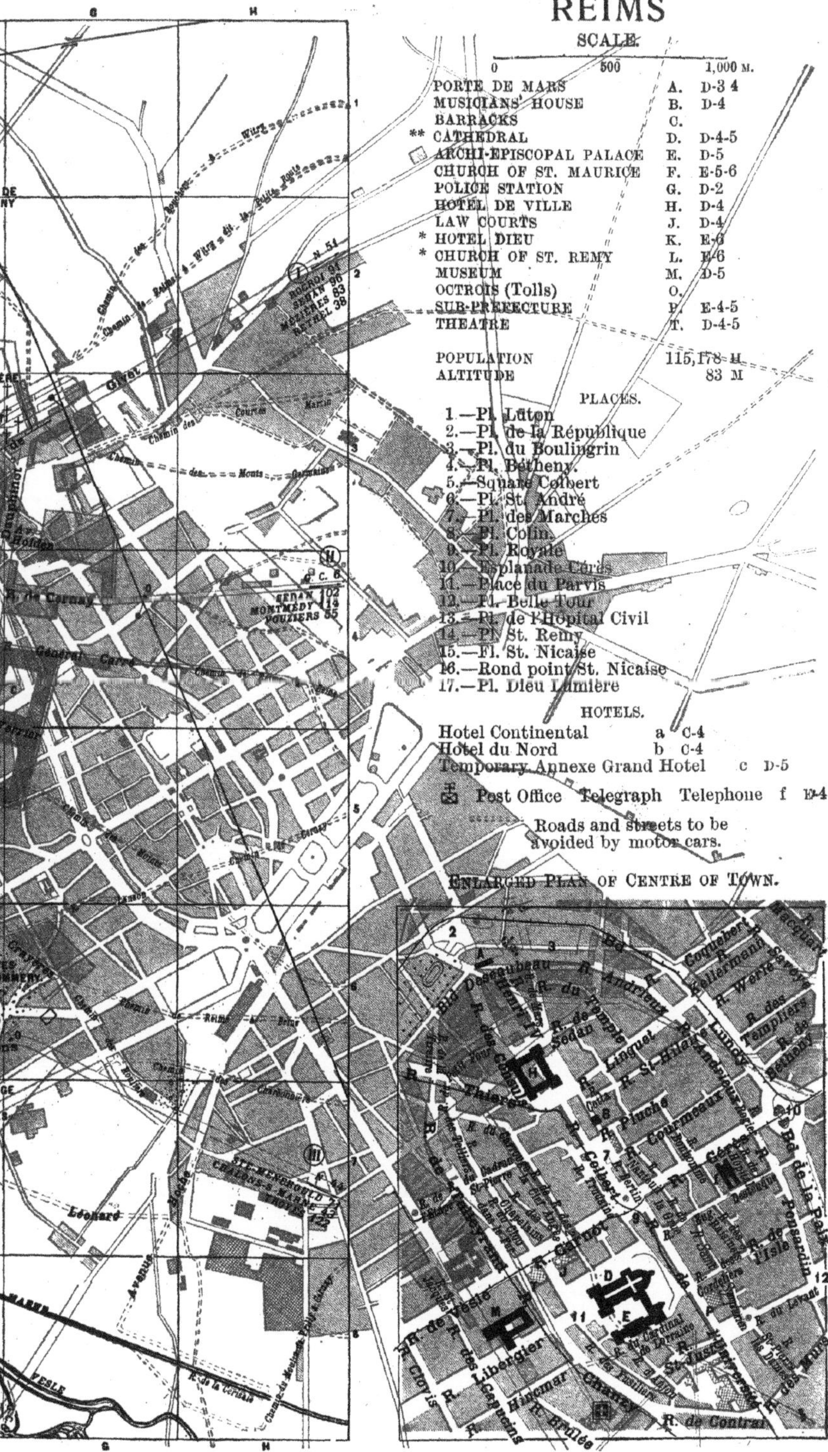
REIMS
SCALE
0 500 1,000 M.
PORTE DE MARS A. D-3 4
MUSICIANS' HOUSE B. D-4
BARRACKS C.
** CATHEDRAL D. D-4-5
ARCHI-EPISCOPAL PALACE E. D-5
CHURCH OF ST. MAURICE F. E-5-6
POLICE STATION G. D-2
HOTEL DE VILLE H. D-4
LAW COURTS J. D-4
* HOTEL DIEU K. E-6
* CHURCH OF ST. REMY L. E-6
MUSEUM M. D-5
OCTROIS (Tolls) O.
SUB-PREFECTURE P. E-4-5
THEATRE T. D-4-5
POPULATION 115,178 H.
ALTITUDE 83 M
PLACES.
1.—Pl. Luton
2.—Pl. de la République
3.—Pl. du Boulingrin
4.—Pl. Betheny.
5.—Square Colbert
6.—Pl. St. André
7.—Pl. des Marchés
8.—Pl. Colin.
9.—Pl. Royale
10.—Esplanade Cérès
11.—Place du Parvis
12.—Pl. Belle Tour
13.—Pl. de l'Hôpital Civil
14.—Pl. St. Remy
15.—Pl. St. Nicaise
16.—Rond point St. Nicaise
17.—Pl. Dieu Lumière
HOTELS.
Hotel Continental a C-4
Hotel du Nord b C-4
Temporary Annexe Grand Hotel c D-5
Post Office Telegraph Telephone f E-4
Roads and streets to be avoided by motor cars.
ENLARGED PLAN OF CENTRE OF TOWN.
G
H
Givet
SEDAN 102
MONTMEDY 114
VOUZIERS 85
ROCROI 91
SEDAN 96
MEZIERES 83
RETHEL 38
N. 51
Léonard
MARNE
VESLE
R. de Cernay
Avenue
R. Andrieux
R. Coquebert
R. Kellermann
R. Werlé
R. des Templiers
R. de Betheny
R. Linguet
R. St-Hilaire
R. Pluche
R. Courmeaux
R. Colbert
R. Cérès
Bd de la Paix
R. Ponsardin
R. de l'Isle
R. Carnot
R. de Vesle
R. Libergier
R. des Capucins
R. Hincmar
R. Brulée
R. Chanzy
R. de Contrai
R. des Murs
R. Clovis
R. Thiers
R. de Sedan
R. du Temple
R. du Levant

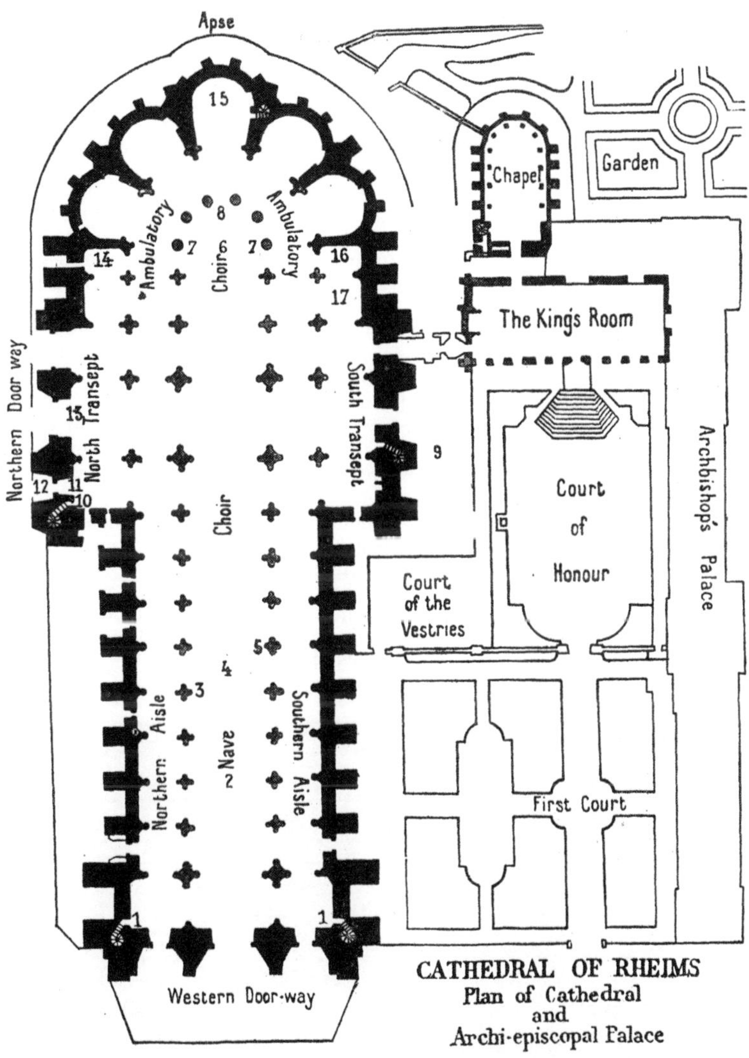

CATHEDRAL OF RHEIMS
Plan of Cathedral
and
Archi-episcopal Palace

1. Staircase of the Towers.
2. Site of the Labyrinth (p. 53).
3. Main Pulpit (p. 53).
4. Site of "La Rouelle de Saint-Nicaise" (Flag-stone with memorial inscription) (p. 53).
5. Pillar supporting the "Vintage Scene" (p. 52).
6. Altar of the Rear Choir (p. 57).
7. 14th century Tombstones (p. 53).
8. Tomb of Cardinal de Lorraine.
9. The Treasure (p. 58).
10. Clock with Automatons (p. 55).
11. Tombstone of Hughes Libergier (p. 55).
12. Norman Door (p. 45).
13. Great Organ (p. 55).
14. Lady Chapel (p. 55).
15. Chapel of the Holy Sacrament (p. 56).
16. Rosary Chapel (p. 57).
17. Roman Mosaic (p. 57).

West Façade

(*See full views on pp.* 28 *and* 29).

Better than any other, this part of the building reveals the desire for unity and harmony which guided the various builders of the Cathedral. The doorway, probably designed by Jean d'Orbais, was very likely not begun till about 1250, by Gaucher, of Rheims. Bernard of Soissons built the great rose-window and the façade as far as the Gallery of the Kings. The architects of the 14th century built the lateral parts forming the first storey of the towers, the Kings' Gallery and the gable. The upper storey of the towers was only finished in the 15th century. Except for slight modifications in detail, the original plan was respected. This façade, with its full open-work towers and immense rose-window, demonstrates that the architects knew how to obtain the maximum of resistance with wonderfully light construction.

The **Western Doorway** (*photo below*) comprises three doors flanked by two full arcades, and surmounted by gables adorned with statues.

Between the gables are pinnacles on small columns (the left-hand ones have been destroyed). At the foot of the pinnacles are statues of seated musicians, which recall those on the house in the Rue de Tambour (*see p.* 80), but which have been partly destroyed.

The splaying of the doors is adorned with great statues backed up against columns and separated by smaller columns, the capitals of which are connected to a foliate frieze of elegant design. The bases are ornamented with carved drapery. The tympana of the doors contain window-lights, while five rows of statues, separated by lines of flowers and foliage, fill up the archings, which suffered severely in the bombardment of September 19, 1914. About a dozen subjects were destroyed or spoilt. During the subsequent bombardments, shell splinters did further damage.

DOORWAY OF THE WEST FRONT BEFORE THE WAR

Generally the sculptural decoration on the ground-floor dates from the middle of the 13th century.

In September, 1914, several of the great statues of the lateral splayings were completely destroyed and the others more or less seriously damaged. However, subsequent damage was slight, thanks to the protective measures taken in 1915.

Central Door

The lavish decoration of the central door suffered mutilations during the last three centuries. The inscription carved on the lintel dates from 1802 and replaced carving descriptive of the life of the Virgin, destroyed during the Revolution. The sculpture on the arches, especially that of the three upper lines. was partly restored in the 17th and 18th centuries.

The beautiful statues in the splayings of the door represent: *to the right* (*photo, p.* 36), the **Annunciation** and **Visitation** (the latter group is striking by reason of its inspiration from the antique); *to the left, the* **Purification** (*photo, p.* 36).

The Virgin of the Annunciation group was damaged by shell splinters on September 4, 1914.

CENTRAL DOOR OF THE WEST FRONT BEFORE THE WAR (*Cliché LL.*)

The Annunciation. *The Visitation.*

RIGHT-HAND SPLAYING OF CENTRAL DOOR

In the gable, a pretty group representing the **Coronation of the Holy Virgin** was injured by the fires of 1914.

Of the two fine statues on the top of the buttresses framing the Central door, only the right-hand one **(Solomon)** exists to-day ; the other, representing the **Queen of Sheba,** was destroyed by a shell in September, 1914, except the head, which was saved.

LEFT-HAND SPLAYING AND LINTEL OF THE CENTRAL DOOR (*Cliché LL.*)

The Right-Hand Door

See photograph on p. 25.

On the lintel, **Saint Paul,** blind, is being led to Ananias, who restores his sight and baptizes him.

On the jambs are pretty little figures which have been variously interpreted. The majority represent vices and virtues, *e.g. on the inner portion :* **Courage,** in knightly raiment ; **Cowardice** fleeing before a hare ; **Charity** holding out a purse ; **Avarice** with a cash-box ; *on the outer portion :* **Pride** blasted and overthrown with his horse ; **Sloth,** represented as a man seated with his head resting on his elbows, in a stall ; **Wisdom** seated, holding a book and a lighted lamp. On the same jambs other figures are supposed to symbolise the seasons: **Autumn** sitting on a vine-trellis ; **Winter** standing before a fire place ; **Spring** in the midst of flowers ; **Summer** with bared chest.

RIGHT-HAND SPLAYING OF THE RIGHT-HAND DOOR
The two central figures have been decapitated.

The six statues in the splaying on the right (*photo above*) represent: the aged **Simeon** holding Christ in his arms; **John the Baptist, Isaiah, Moses** with the brazen serpent and the tables of the Law; **Abraham** about to sacrifice Isaac; **Samuel** carrying a lamb (which has been broken). They differ by their more archaic style from the other sculptures of the lower façade, and closely resemble those of the central door of the north transept of the Cathedral of Chartres. Like the latter, they date without doubt from the beginning of the 13th century. Possibly they belonged to an earlier doorway, or were prepared in advance for a purpose not realised, being finally utilised in the place where they now stand.

The **Last Judgment,** in the gable, was severely damaged by shell splinters.

The Left-Hand Door

This door, on account of the scaffolding which surrounded it, was seriously damaged by the fires of September, 1914 (*see p.* 17).

On the lintel is **Saint Paul,** thrown from his horse at the gates of Damascus. On the outside of the jambs, fourteen seated figures meditating, are supposed by some to be embodiments of the arts and sciences, but represent more probably prophets or teachers. Along the splayings are eleven statues, which have not definitely been identified.

In the left-hand splaying is **Saint Nicaise** between two angels. The right-hand angel, generally known as the **"Smile of Rheims,"** was decapitated on September 19, 1914. Fortunately, the fragments of the head of this fine statue were saved.

The sculptures in the archings depict scenes from the Passion, while the group which adorns the gable represents **The Crucifixion.**

These archings and gable were greatly damaged by the fires of September 19, 1914, and the bombardments.

LEFT-HAND DOOR OF THE WEST FRONT

The headless angel on the left against the door was known as the "Smile of Rheims."

LEFT-HAND SPLAYING OF THE LEFT-HAND DOOR, BEFORE THE WAR

St. Nicaise (between two angels) and St. Clotilda. The angel on the right, known as the "Smile of Rheims," was decapitated. (See photo, p. 38.) Cliché LL.

GABLE OF THE LEFT-HAND DOOR, WITH CRUCIFIXION

(Cliché LL.)

FIRST STOREY OF THE WEST FRONT

The First Storey

In the centre is the great rose-window, best seen from the interior of the nave. The stained-glass is broken. On either side, against the arching which surmounts it, were two large statues. One of them, *David as a youth in shepherd's garb* (also known as the *Pilgrim*), was destroyed by the bombardments. The other very fine statue is variously said to be *Saul, Solomon* and *St. James.*

The arching which begins above these statues was adorned with small groups of figures representing scenes from the life of Solomon. Most of them were destroyed at the same time as the Pilgrim statue.

Above the arching, a gigantic statue (twice restored) represents *David challenging Goliath.* The bombardments of 1914 destroyed a similar statue on the left representing *David slaying Goliath with a stone from his sling.*

The first storey of the towers flanking the rose-window is broken by lofty twin bays crowned with gables. The niches and pinnacles of the buttresses are identical with those of the nave, but the style of their decoration denotes a more recent period (early 14th century).

The northern tower was badly damaged by the bombardment of September 19, 1914, which fired the scaffolding around it (*see photo, p.* 9). Two of the pinnacled niches surmounting the buttresses were decapitated, while the flames completely disfigured the statues, including that of Christ.

A large calibre shell burst in the southern tower on April 19, 1917, causing very serious damage.

SECOND STOREY AND UPPER STOREY OF THE TOWERS

The Second Storey

The second storey comprises a series of niches, surmounted by sharply pointed gables and adorned with gigantic statues, known as the *Kings' Gallery.*

The central group, consisting of seven figures, commemorates the *Baptism of Clovis.* Clovis, standing in the baptismal font, between Saint Remi, receiving the Sacred Ampulla, and Clotilda.

The balcony in front of the *Baptism of Clovis* was formerly called the *Gloria Gallery,* as it was the custom for the choir-boys to sing the *Gloria* there on Palm Sunday.

The Upper Portion of the Towers

The upper storey of the towers, built on an octagonal plan, is flanked with four open-work turrets, one of which contains stairs leading to the platforms.

The northern tower, badly damaged by the fire of 1914, lost several of the fine colonnettes of its corner turrets in 1918.

In the same year, the pierced staircase of the southern tower was almost entirely destroyed.

At the time of the last restorations, the foundations of the spires provided for in the original plans, but which have never been built, were laid.

In the belfry of the northern tower are two magnificent deep-toned bells. One of them is modern and was cast at Le Mans, and blessed in 1849 by Cardinal Gousset. The other, one of the finest bells known, and presented to the church in 1570 by Cardinal Charles de Lorraine, is the work of the Rheims metal-founder, Pierre Deschamps.

The scaffolding fire of 1914 reached the belfry, bringing down the bells, which were broken in the fall.

The Lateral Façades and Chevet

The lateral façades of the Cathedral are of rare beauty Nowhere have abutments and flying buttresses been so harmoniously employed as here. They are not merely supports, but form part of the decorative scheme of the nave, and ensure the harmony of the whole. Buttresses, finished off with pinnacles, serve as points of support for two superimposed flying-buttresses. The octagonal pinnacles are flanked with four small triangular pyramids and supported in front by two slender detached columns. Between the latter, under canopies, angels with outstretched wings carry the instruments of the Passion and various other emblems (*see photo, p.* 49).

Skirt the Cathedral on the left, passing in front of the North Façade (see photo below), to reach the Northern Transept.

THE NORTHERN TRANSEPT IN 1919

The Northern Façade and Transept

The transept is pierced with broad bays, whose completion, as in all the windows of the Cathedral, consists of two twin arches surmounted by a six-leaved rose. The niches in the buttresses are ornamented with statues believed by some to represent Kings of France. At any rate, that of the buttress on the western fro t of the north-west tower greatly resembles the figure of St. Louis carved on the doorway of the church of St. Vincent at Carcassonne.

The carvings of the lower windows were either destroyed or damaged on September 19, 1914, at the same time as the stained-glass. The two towers which flank the crossings were left unfinished.

Before the fire of 1481, there was a lantern over the intersection of the transept.

CENTRAL DOOR OF THE NORTHERN TRANSEPT

The Central Door of the Northern Transept

The sculptural decoration, while rich, is more sober than that of the doorway of the western façade. It is commemorative of the glory of the Archbishops of Rheims.

The statue of the Pontiff with a tiara, backing up to the dividing-pillar, is supposed to be that of St. Sixtus, first Bishop of Rheims. In the splaying, on the left, is St Nicaise holding his head in his hands, between St Eutropia, an angel and a figure improbably said to be Clovis.

The pediment was pierced by a shell and scarred with splinters. It is divided into five tiers, and represent the life of St. Remi and St. Nicaise

Beginning at the bottom, the figures represent: *on the first tier*, the beheading of St. Nicaise by the Vandals and the Baptism of Clovis by St. Remi; *on the second*, St. Remi, as a child, restores sight to Montanus and, as a man, exorcises the demons who had set fire to Rheims; *on the third*, the story of Job; *on the fourth*, the restoring to life of a young Toulouse girl, and the miracle of the cask filled with wine by St. Remi; *on the fifth*, Christ between two angels.

LEFT-HAND DOOR OF THE NORTHERN TRANSEPT : THE LAST JUDGMENT
The dead rise from their graves.

The Left-Hand Door of the Northern Transept

This door, which has long been walled up, is called *The Doorway of the Last Judgment,* on account of the carving on the tympanum.

In the upper part, Christ is supported on one side by the Holy Virgin, and on the other by John the Baptist. Below (*two rows*) the dead rise from their graves (*photo above*). Lower down, on one side are *The Virtues*, represented by seated women ; on the other, *The Vices*, mutilated in 1780 on account of their realism. On the lowest tier, *to the left*, angels carry souls to Abraham's bosom ; *on the right*, Satan leads a chain of damned souls to Hell (*photo below*), amongst whom are a king, a bishop, and a monk.

In the arching are three rows of angels carrying books or blowing trumpets, and the wise and foolish virgins.

Backing up to the dividing pillar is an exceedingly fine 13th century statue, which recalls the "*Beautiful God*" of Amiens Cathedral (*see the Michelin Guide : Amiens Before and During the War*) ; Jesus blessing with His right hand, holds the globe of the world in His left (*see photo p.* 45).

This statue was decapitated by a shell which struck the doorway in 1918, also taking off the head of the first statue on the left-hand portion of the doorway.

LEFT-HAND DOOR OF THE NORTHERN TRANSEPT : THE LAST JUDGMENT
Satan drags a chain of damned Souls to Hell.

On the plinth of the dividing pillar is a bas-relief, remarkable for its delicate carving.

According to local tradition, this plinth was erected at the expense of a dishonest master-draper, convicted of selling by false measure.

On the left, the merchant is seen in his shop. In front of the counter, customers of both sexes look at the outspread stuffs, while clerks write in books.

On the right, the merchant kneels before a statue of the Vi gin in penance.

Near-by, burgesses talk together and seem to judge the delinquent's conduct severely.

The six statues against the walls represent the apostles: *on the right,* St. John, St James and St. Paul; *on the left,* St. Andrew, St. Peter and St. Bartholomew.

DIVIDING-PILLAR OF THE LEFT-HAND DOOR OF THE NORTHERN TRANSEPT

The statue of Christ was decapitated by a shell.

On the plinth is the legend of the Master-draper (see text opposite).

The rose is carved in a voussoir; the uprights are decorated with statues of Adam and Eve in long tunics, and the arch with twenty-two groups of small figures depicting, *from left to right,* the story of Adam and Eve, the various tasks to which they and their descendants were condemned, and the story of Cain and Abel.

Above the rose an open-work gallery contains seven statues of the prophets. The statues are 13th century, but the gallery was restored in 1846.

The balustrading and triangular gable flanked with pinnacles, which dominate the gallery, date from the beginning of the 16th century, but have been repaired in recent times. On the gable is a colossal **Annunciation;** the Archangel and Mary are under Flamboyant canopies.

The Right-Hand Door of the Northern Transept (Norman Door)

This little door formerly connected, by means of a vaulted passage, the Cathedral with the Cloister (no longer existing) of the Chapter.

Its tympanum is a relic of the Cathedral built by Archbishop Samson. It depicts, in beautiful Romanesque relief, a majestic Virgin. The archivolt which frames it, doubtless belonged to a 12th century tomb. At the top of the arch, angels carry away a soul, while on the uprights, clerks officiate at a funeral service.

The Chevet

(*See photograph of Cathedral, taken from aeroplane, p.* 30.)

The Chevet, begun by Jean D'Orbais and finished by Jean Le Loup, was inaugurated by the Chapter about 1241. It is one of the finest 13th century chevets in existence.

It is stayed by two rows of buttresses supporting double flying-buttresses. Like those of the nave, the buttresses are surmounted with pinnacles, beneath which niches shelter statues of flying angels.

THE CHEVET BEFORE THE WAR

One of the finest 13th century Chevets.

All around the apse, between the windows of the radial chapels and on the main buttresses, are statues of angels, some of them of great beauty.

The 13th century clerestory gallery, which surrounds the upper portion of the apsidal chapels, was restored by Viollet-le-Duc. It was partially destroyed by the bombardments. On April 19, 1917, three large calibre shells, which burst on the chevet, destroyed forty to fifty feet of it. At the same time, the buttress jutting on the centre of the destroyed gallery lost its pinnacle, and behind, an arch of the flying-buttress. The buttresses between the above-mentioned one and the corner of the South Transept Tower lost either a colonnette or their pinnacle with angel statue.

The slender spire which, before the War, rose above the chevet, was known as the **Angel Spire,** on account of a bronze angel which surmounted it, and which was removed in 1860 as unsafe This spire, the work of Colard le Moine, was built in 1485, after the fire of 1481. Its pierced base with balustrading was supported by eight leaden caryatids, some of which, in the popular costume of the Louis XI. period, became deformed in consequence of the rotting of their oaken core.

The fire of September 19, 1914, caused by the German shells, entirely destroyed the spire and its caryatids.

THE CHEVET IN 1919

The roof with the "Angel Spire" was destroyed.

The bombardments in the spring of the following year further damaged the gallery, also causing fresh mutilations to the flying buttresses and the pinnacles of the apse.

A plain stone gallery with blind arcading, which formerly ran round the chevet on a level with the springing of the roof, was replaced by Viollet-le-Duc, with pierced battlemented arcading. Part of the original gallery which surrounded the entire building, level with the roof, still exists on the northern side.

On October 12, 1914, a shell destroyed about twenty-five feet of the gallery round the chevet, which later was further damaged by another shell.

The Lateral Façade and South Transept

This façade and transept (*which should be seen from the courtyard of the Archbishop's Palace*) are identical, as a whole, with the northern façade and transept (*see pp.* 28 *and* 42).

The gallery at the springing of the roof of the nave was entirely rebuilt in 1878 by Architect Millet, in a style foreign to that of the Cathedral.

Among the statues of the transept buttresses that at the corner of the south-western tower, bestriding a lion, is thought by some to represent **Pepin-the-Short,** and another near him, **Charlemagne.**

THE LATERAL FAÇADE AND SOUTHERN TRANSEPT IN 1919

The façade of the transept has no doorway. Above the lower storey, the architectural arrangement is the same as that of the northern transept. At the base of the rose-window, on each side, are two very fine statues.

On the left, **The Christian Religion,** symbolised by a crowned woman with chalice and standard. This statue was destroyed by a German shell in 1918, after being damaged in April 1917.

On the right, **The Synagogue,** with eyes bandaged and a crown on one side, was not seriously damaged.

In consequence of the fire of 1481, the gable of the South Transept was rebuilt at the beginning of the 16th century by three master-masons, one of whom, Guichart Antoine, co-operated later with the building of **Notre-Dame de l'Epine.** *(See the Michelin Guide: The Revigny Pass.)* It was restored about 1888 in the original style. The subject sculptured on the pediment represents the **Assumption of the Virgin.**

The **Sagittarius** which surmounted the gable was destroyed in 1914. It was a modern faithful copy of the old lead-covered wooden Sagittarius, which was carved, gilded and painted about 1503 by the Rheims sculptor, Jean Bourcamus. According to tradition, this Sagittarius, which appeared to be shooting its arrow at the bronze stag of the archi-episcopal palace, symbolised the rivalry between the Archbishop and the Chapter of the Cathedral

GABLE OF THE SOUTHERN TRANSEPT IN 1914

THE SOUTHERN LATERAL FAÇADE IN 1914

REVERSE SIDE OF THE CENTRAL DOOR IN 1914

See complete view on p. 52.

THE INTERIOR OF THE CATHEDRAL

The Inner Western Façade

(*See description of the Exterior on pp.* 34 *to* 41.)

This is a master-piece. Its sculptural decoration is unique, and as rich as that of the outer façade.

In the tympanum of the central door a sixteen-leaved rose-window, the stained-glass of which was made shortly before the Revolution, is faced with three small trefoil rose-windows.

At the top of the dividing pillar St. Nicaise, headless, is between two angels and two armed men personifying the barbarians who killed him.

The entire door, as far as the triforium, is framed by seven rows of superimposed niches separated by panels of sculptured foliage. The basements are covered with figured drapery, as on the outside. In each niche, under a trefoil arcade, is a statue The subjects represented are, *from bottom to top :*

STATUES ON REVERSE SIDE OF DOORS AFTER FIRE, SEPT., 1914

on the right : **The Life of John the Baptist;** *on the left :* **The Fulfilment of the Prophecy** and **The Childhood of Christ.**

The first row on the right is known as **"The Knight's Communion";** a priest offers the Host to a knight wearing 13th century armour, and turns his back on another knight clothed in a leathern Carolingian tunic with iron scales, and armed with a small round buckler.

Above the door, a gallery with nine openings lights the triforium.

On the highest storey, the great rose-window occupies the whole breadth of the nave. It is the masterpiece of Bernard de Soissons (*see p.* 40).

In the form of a gigantic flower with twelve petals, each of the latter is sub-divided by quatrefoils and trefoil archings. Its harmonious gracefulness and seeming lightness, in spite of the great thickness of its border (about 7 ft.), and mullions (about 2 ft. 6 in.), are very striking.

The stained-glass, which, with the stonework, formed a harmonious whole, was restored in modern times. The subject represented was: **The Virgin surrounded by angels, kings and patriarchs.**

The fire of 1914 destroyed the stained-glass.

The side-doors have only a quatrefoil rose-window (*see pp.* 25 *and* 34), and their framework of niches consists only of four rows of two niches each. However, two lines of niches, in which are statues in demi-relief, form the contour of the arches which frame their top.

The subjects of the sculptures are allied, in the case of each door, to those of the outer decoration, *i.e.* **"The Life of St. Stephen."**

The wooden doors and their tambours were destroyed by the fire of September 19, 1914, which also disfigured or destroyed the statues framing them (*see photos above*).

INTERIOR OF THE NAVE IN 1919

The Great Nave

The fire of September 19, 1914, destroyed the framework of the Nave and its 15th century lead roof. In the following years a number of shells pierced the vaulting, without, however, damaging its vital parts. It will be possible to restore it.

It seems to be clearly established that although the first four bays were built later than the others, the nave as a whole, like that of the Cathedral of Amiens, was completely finished before 1300 A.D. Vaulted throughout on diagonal ribs, the nave, which is perfectly regular, has three stories: the lowest, formed of great arches, rests on massive pillars; the triforium, formed of two, four, five, or six arcades, extends round the entire building; the high twin-bay windows are surmounted with a six-leaved rose-window.

The pillars, which have been likened to a row of antique columns, are composed of a great cylindrical shaft, reinforced by four smaller engaged columns, standing on an octagonal base. The pillars which follow the first bay of the nave and carry one of the corners of the towers, as also the four pillars of the transept square, are more massive.

CAPITAL IN THE NAVE

The capitals of the pillars and of the columns (*photo opposite*) are most beautifully decorated. The dominating subject of their decoration is natural foliage (vine, oak, thistle, ivy, ranunculus, fig-tree). Occasionally, human or animal figures or monsters, and scenes from nature, *i.e.* the dainty **Vintage scene** on the capital of the sixth pillar on the right of the nave, are interspersed. The ornamentation of the capitals of six pillars of the first bays is more elaborate and more recent in style. These capitals are not, like those of the other pillars, divided on the four flanking columns into two equal courses by an astragal, neither do they include, like some of the others, crockets, acanthus leaves and other conventional ornaments of an older and less realistic style.

The 13th and 14th century stained-glass of the high windows represents, on two superimposed lines, figures of kings of France and archbishops of Rheims. Some of the glass was broken, but the finest was saved.

In the third and fourth bays there was formerly a square **Labyrinth,** flanked at the corners by polygonal compartments. In the interior, a line of white tiles bordered with black stones ran from one side, and after complicated windings reached a central compartment. At the corners of the compartments were figures of the four first architects of the Cathedral: Jean d'Orbais, Jean le Loup, Gaucher of Rheims and Bernard of Soissons. The central figure is probably that of Archbishop Aubri de Humbert, who laid the first stone of the edifice. This Labyrinth, the drawings of which revealed the names of the builders of the Cathedral, was destroyed in 1778 by the Chapter, to prevent the children playing there.

Between the Labyrinth and the Choir are about twenty 14th century tombstones.

The **great pulpit** set up against the fifth left-hand pillar was made, in the time of Louis XV., by a Rheims artist (Blondel). It comes from the old church of St. Pierre-le-Vieil.

In the sixth bay, just before

ROOF OF THE NAVE IN 1914

In the foreground on the right: Corner of the Southern Transept.

ROOF OF THE NAVE IN 1919

In the foreground, on the right: Corner of the Southern Transept.

the entrance to the choir, the spot where St. Nicaise was beheaded, on the threshold of his church, was formerly indicated by a small circular chapel known as *La Rouelle de St. Nicaise.* The tiny building was replaced by a memorial inscription on the flagstone, supposed to have been stained with the blood of the martyr.

The Aisles of the Naves

The windows of the Aisles are similar to the lofty windows of the nave. The walls were formerly hung with valuable tapestries, which were taken down and evacuated by the *Historical Monuments Department* at the outbreak of the War. The two oldest, dating back to about 1440, and known as the tapestries of the *fort roi Clovis,* were presented by Cardinal Charles de Lorraine, and depict the history of Clovis. Those of the Renaissance, given in 1530 by Archbishop Robert de Lenoncourt, who caused himself to be portrayed kneeling in the picture of the Birth of Christ, depict the *Life of the Virgin.* The most modern, presented in 1640 by Archbishop Henri de Lorraine and worked by the Fleming, Daniel Pepersack, represent Jesus at the *Marriage at Cana in Galilee* and *Jesus among the Doctors.*

At the foot of the walls, three stone steps serve as seats.

TAPESTRIES IN THE SOUTHERN SIDE AISLE, BEFORE THE WAR

The Interior of the Northern Transept

(*See plan, p. 33, and the Exterior, p. 42.*)

The inner façade is partially hidden by the great organ, built about 1487 and transformed several times since then. Of the original organ the loft only remains, the Gothic balustrading of which is pierced with Flamboyant arcading.

The façade originally consisted of three lofty bays with lancet-shaped windows surmounted by a gallery lighted by three rose-windows of six lobes each and one of twelve lobes. The subsequent addition of a doorway about the *middle* of the 13th century caused the partial suppression of the bays, of which the transformed summits alone remain.

Almost all the high windows of the transept contained 13th century *grisaille* glass, which was damaged or broken by the bombardments, as was also the 13th century stained-glass of the great rose-window (repaired in 1869), which represented *The Story of the Creation* and *The Fall of Adam.*

THE NORTHERN TRANSEPT (*see p.* 33)

The reverse side of the Central Door is bare, except the dividing pillar, the statue of which is hidden by the 18th century wooden tambour.

The small western side-door, which formerly communicated with the cloister of the Chapter, is entirely covered with 18th century woodwork. The adjoining bay, closed in by a beautiful 13th century wrought-iron railling, is the old chartulary or muniment room of the Chapter. Near the railing, in the corner of the transept, is a clock with automatons, which come out when the hours strike. Its woodwork is 14th and 15th century and its works 17th and 18th century.

To the right of the door of the organ stair, a **tombstone** to **Hugues Libergier** was set up against the wall. He was the architect who, in 1231, commenced the abbatial church of St. Nicaise. The tombstone has been in the Cathedral since 1800. The altar in the Lady-Chapel, surmounted with a statue by François Ladatte (1742), replaced a Gothic altar-screen destroyed in 1739.

The picture *The Washing of the Disciples' Feet* is by Jerome Muziano.

On the western walls of the transept is a fine tapestry, the pendant of which is in the south transept. These two great tapestries, made at the Gobelins, after cartoons by Raphael, represent the life of St. Paul. They were removed in 1914, at the same time as those in the aisles.

THE VAULTING OF THE CHOIR FELL IN ON THE HIGH ALTAR
The photo on p. 31 shows the collapse, seen from above.

The Choir

(*See the Chevet, p.* 46.)

The ambulatory with its radiating chapels is of incomparable beauty. Excepting the larger central chapel, known as the *Chapel of the Holy Sacrament*, which is nine-sided, each chapel has seven sides rising from a circular floor.

In each chapel, three windows similar to those of the nave, light the three hindmost walls. Blind windows imitate the true ones on the side walls.

At the base of the windows a narrow gallery, passing through the pillars, continues all along the side-aisles of the transept and nave—a peculiarity in Champagne architecture.

The 13th century stained-glass of the high windows was destroyed by the bombardment of September 19, 1914.

In April, 1917, part of the vaulting fell in on the High Altar (*photo above*).

The costly marble High Altar was erected in 1747 by Canon Godinot, who spent considerable sums in making alterations to the Cathedral, not all of which were happy. Its six chandeliers date from the consecration of Charles X.

The High Altar of the rear choir dates from 1764 and came from the Church of St. Nicaise. On either side of this altar are two 14th century tumulary stones. Behind is the tomb of Cardinal de Lorraine.

The small pulpit of the rear choir, the medallions of which depict the life of St. Theresa, dates from 1678. It is a gift of the widow of M. Pommery (*photo below*).

Twenty-two archbishops of Rheims were buried under the choir pavement. Their tombstones were removed in 1747. The present flag-stones came from the old church of St. Nicaise.

THE SMALL PULPIT IN THE REAR CHOIR

The archbishop's throne, by Viollet-le-Duc, was destroyed by the fire of 1914, together with the 18th century stalls.

The railings (1826–1832) replaced, not very happily, an ancient stone rood-loft destroyed in 1761.

The Interior of the Southern Transept

(*See plan, p.* 33, *and the Exterior, p.* 47)

A gap was made in the vaulting by the bombardment of April 19, 1917.

The arrangement of the inner façade is similar to that of the northern transept, except that the three high bays with lancet windows, which are partially hidden in the northern transept, are here entirely visible.

The stained-glass of the rose-window, destroyed by a hurricane in 1580, was replaced in 1581 by the Rheims artist Nicolas Dérodé. It represents the Eternal Father surrounded by the twelve apostles.

In the Rosary Chapel is a Renaissance altar-screen (1541), attributed to the Rheims sculptor Pierre Jacques. The general scheme represents *The dead body of Christ on the knees of the Virgin,* and above, *Christ coming forth from the sepulchre.* It was a gift of Canon Paul Grandraoul, who is shown on his knees before Mary Magdalene.

The Roman mosaic work in the centre of the chapel was discovered in the courtyard of the archbishop's palace in 1849. Among the most remarkable scenes are : *Christ appearing to Mary Magdalene,* attributed to Titian ; *Christ with the angels,* by Thaddeo Zuccaro ; *The Nativity,* attributed to Tintoret ; *Manna in the Desert,* attributed to Nicolas Poussin.

ST. REMI'S CHALICE. (*Cliché LL.*)

The Cathedral Treasure

This is kept in a sacristy built by Viollet-le-Duc, which is reached through a plain door in the southern façade of the transept.

The treasure, which is very rich in precious reliquaries, chalices, and other pieces of goldsmith's work, was saved from the fire of September 19, 1914, by the Curé of the Cathedral and one of his abbés. After being temporarily placed in the house of the Cardinal, it was evacuated in 1915, at the order of the Historical Monuments Department.

Among the best known of these art treasures are the Chalice of St. Remi and St. Ursula's Skiff.

The **Chalice of St. Remi,** with its gold filagree work, six rows of chasing, and precious stones set in a *collier*, is a remarkab'e work of art. It was in this chalice that, by special privilege, the kings of France communicated in wine at the conclusion of their consecration. Tradition has it that the gold

ST. URSULA'S SKIFF. (*Cliché L.L.*)

of which it is made was that of the Soissons Vase, whereas in reality it is 12th century. Confiscated in 1793 and deposited in the *Bibliothèque Nationale,* it was restored to the Cathedral by Napoleon III.

St. Ursula's Skiff is a reliquary given by Henri III. It represents a ship carved out of cornelian, floating on a sea of enamel. The ship, whose mast bears the royal crown, is adorned with the escutcheons of France and Poland, and contains eleven small figures. That of St. Ursula is said to be the portrait of the Queen of France.

Amongst the other remarkable works of art in the Treasure are the following: the *reliquaries* of Archbishop Samson, St. Sixtus (12th century), St. Peter and St. Paul (14th century), and the Holy Sepulchre (16th century); a *monstrance* of gilt copper (13th century); a *liturgical comb* of ivory, said to have belonged to St. Bernard (12th century); a rock-crystal *cross,* which formerly belonged to Cardinal de Lorraine; *orfrays* embroidered with silver thread (13th century); the *credence* and *oil vessels* of Abbot de la Salle; a *fragment* of a carved wood crozier (incorrectly said to be the crozier of

CASKET OF THE SACRED AMPULLA. (*Cliché LL.*)

St. Gibrien), two other fragments of which are in the Town Museum (12th century); the *vases, utensils,* and *sacred ornaments* which were used at the consecration of Charles X.; the *reliquary* of the Sacred Ampulla, designed by Lafitte for the consecration of Charles X. The original Sacred Ampulla was broken in 1793. The present one, which has only served for the consecration of Charles X., is a replica said to have been made with the few drops of balsam of the Clovis Ampulla, which pious hands saved from the broken fragments of the sacred vessel.

FRAGMENTS SAVED FROM THE RUINS. (*Cliché LL.*)

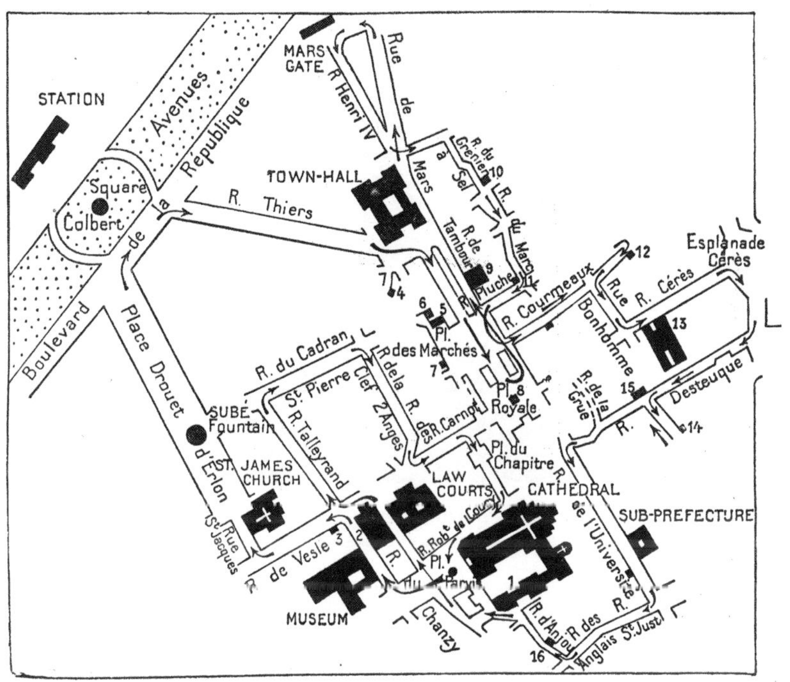

FIRST ITINERARY FOR VISITING RHEIMS

Starting-point: Place du Parvis Notre-Dame

1. The Archbishop's Palace (p. 63).
2. The Theatre (p. 68)
3. The House of Levesque de Pouilly (p. 68).
4. The Stores: Galeries Rémoises (p. 73).
5. The Maison Fossier (p. 75).
6. The House of J. B. de la Salle (p. 75).
7. The House of the Enfant d'Or (p. 75).
8. The Statue of Louis XV. (p. 79).
9. The Musicians' House (p. 80).
10. The House of De Muire (p. 83).
11. The House of Le Vergeur (p. 85).
12. A 16th Century House (p. 86).
13. The General Post Office and Chamber of Commerce (p. 87).
14. The Cloister of the Franciscan Friars (p. 90).
15. The House of Thiret de Prain (p. 89).
16. The House of de la Pourcelette (p. 92).

REMOVING THE STATUE OF JOAN-OF-ARC
IN MAY, 1918

Place du Parvis

The Place du Parvis (*photo below*) is in front of the main façade of the Cathedral. The shells made enormous craters there.

In the centre of the square stands an **equestrian statue of Joan-of-Arc,** by Paul Dubois, of which there is a replica in the Place St. Augustin in Paris. It was removed in May, 1918, by the Historical Monuments Department (*photo above*).

THE PLACE DU PARVIS

On the right : The Law Courts. In the centre : The Theatre. On the left : The Grand Hôtel. In centre of Square : Statue of Joan-of-Arc.

Looking towards the Cathedral, the tourist will see on the right the ruins of the *Hôtel du Lion d'Or* and of the *Hôtel de la Maison Rouge.*

The latter was completely destroyed. Above the door was the inscription: "In the year 1429, at the consecration of Charles VII., in this hostelry—then called the 'Striped Ass'—the father and mother of Jeanne d'Arcq were lodged at the expense of the Municipality." In reality only the father of Joan-of-Arc lodged there.

It was at the Hôtel du Lion d'Or (*photo opposite*) and at the Grand Hôtel (No. 4 in the Rue Libergier, which opens out in front of the statue of Joan-of-Arc) that the Field-Marshal French stayed in August, 1914, and later General von Zuchow, commanding the Saxon troops which entered Rheims on September 4, 1914.

On the right of the Cathedral are the ruins of the Archbishop's Palace (*see plan, p.* 33). A general view of them is seen in the photograph on p. 48.

INNER COURTYARD OF THE LION D'OR HÔTEL. (*Cliché A.S.*)

The Archbishop's Palace

Of the three buildings which surrounded every Cathedral in the Middle Ages—the bishop's palace, the cloister of the canons, and the house set apart for the sick and poor (Hôtel-Dieu) – only the archbishop's palace existed at Rheims in 1914. It extended all along the south lateral façade of the Cathedral, on the site of the ancient abode of St. Nicaise, which had replaced a Roman palace. Of the ancient building erected by the successors of St. Nicaise down to the 13th century, there remained only the graceful two-storied chapel, doubtless contemporary with the chevet of the Cathedral. The round entrance tower, known as Eon's tower (from the name of the heretic who was imprisoned there in the 12th century), and the great bronze stag placed in the middle of the courtyard by Archbishop Samson in the 11th century, still existed in the 17th century, but about that time the one was demolished and the other melted down. This stag, into which on feast-days wine was poured, which flowed out again by the mouth, was a beautiful specimen of the art of the old metal-founders of Rheims.

The archbishop's palace and most of its rich collections were burnt in the fire of September 19, 1914. Of the palace proper there remains only the great chimney-piece of the Salle du Tau, on which the Latin motto, "Good faith preserved makes rich," is inscribed (*see p.* 64), the very opposite of the German "scrap of paper" theory.

The Archevêché: The buildings which lined the courtyard were of different periods. The wing abutting on the entrance-gate was 19th century, while the correct but heavy and dull southern façade was rebuilt in the 17th century by Archbishop Maurice Le Tellier, from the plans of Robert de Cotte.

THE SALLE DU TAU, BEFORE THE WAR

The Salle du Tau (or Kings' Hall)

(*See plan, p.* 33.)

At the bottom of the courtyard there used to be a large late 15th and early 16th century hall, access to which was gained by a horse-shoe stair with late 17th century wrought-iron hand-rail.

A small porch-like structure at the top of the stair was an unfortunate addition of 1825.

The hall was known as the **Salle du Tau,** in memory of the ancient palace which was shaped like the Greek letter *Tau*, or the Kings' Hall, on account of the portraits of the Kings consecrated at Rheims, received in 1825.

Built by the Cardinal Archbishop Guillaume Briçonnet between 1497 and 1507, it comprised two stories.

THE SALLE DU TAU IN 1918

Behind the ruined Hall are seen the Southern Transept and Chevet of the Cathedral.

The upper hall, in which the royal banquet was served at the consecrations, became the Stock Exchange at the beginning of the 19th century. It was disfigured by poor paintings and false Gothic ornamentation at the time of the consecration of Charles X.

The walls were hung with four admirable tapestries by Pepersack and several others given by Robert de Lenoncourt.

The vast chimney-piece with the Briçonnet and Church of Rheims Arms is all that the fire of 1914 spared of the ancient decoration. It is visible in the photographs on page 64, at the bottom of the hall.

The lower hall, with its Gothic arching, was as large as the upper one. The capitals of the prismatic pillars and the key-stones of the arches were adorned with escutcheons, fleur-de-lys, flowers and crockets.

ENTRANCE TO THE SALLE DU TAU (OR KINGS' HALL). (*See plan, p.* 33.)

The Archi-episcopal Chapel

(*See plan, p.* 33.)

This was without doubt the work of Jean d'Orbais, the first architect of the Cathedral. It resembled the latter in many respects.

With its seven-sided apse, four-bay nave and lancet-shaped windows without rubber-work, it was remarkably slender and graceful.

Its finest ornament was the 13th century bas-relief, *The Adoration of the Magi*, in the tympanum of the entrance door.

The white marble inner portico of the door dated from the Restoration The other, formed of in-laid wood panels, was adorned with five 16th or early 17th century painted figures.

The lower chapel, partly subterranean, was fitted up as a lapidary museum in 1865 and 1896.

ENTRANCE TO THE ARCHI-EPISCOPAL CHAPEL. (*See plan, p.* 33.)

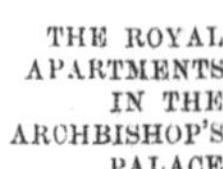

THE ROYAL APARTMENTS IN THE ARCHBISHOP'S PALACE

The Royal Apartments

From the Kings' Hall, access was obtained to five royal saloons with windows looking on the gardens and adorned with portraits of archbishops.

It was in the archbishop's palace that the Kings stayed at the time of their consecration or when passing through Rheims. Henry IV. lived there during his two sojourns at Rheims. He washed the feet of the poor on Holy Thursday in the great hall and listened to the sermon of Father Cotton. Louis XIII. and Richelieu stayed there in 1641, Louis XIV. in 1680, Peter the Great in 1717, Louis XV. in 1722 and 1744, the Queen in 1765, Louis XVI. and Marie Antoinette in 1774, and Charles X. in 1825. From year VI. (Revolution Calendar) to 1824 it was occupied by the tribunals. The archbishops formerly held many Councils and Synods there, but lived there only rarely. In the Middle Ages they preferred living in their fortified castle of Porte Mars (*see p. 6*). In the 17th and 18th centuries they lived mostly outside Rheims.

After visiting the ruins of the Archbishop's Palace return to the Place du Parvis. Take the Rue Libergier, opposite the Cathedral, turning into the first street on the right (*Rue Chanzy*). *The Museum is soon reached* (*see Itinerary, p. 61*).

The Museum, formerly **The Grand Séminaire**

This fine 18th century building was erected by Nicolas Bonhomme in 1743-1752. The carved entrance-door and terraced central pavilion, bordered with a fine balustrade (damaged by shell splinters), are the remains of the ancient Abbey of St. Denis, the church of which was destroyed at the time of the Revolution. The right wing was rebuilt in the 19th century, by order of Cardinal Thomas Gousset. The ground-floor of the left wing is old, but

THE ENTRANCE TO THE COURT-YARD OF THE OLD GRAND SÉMINAIRE (18th century)

the other floors are modern. These buildings were comparatively little damaged by the bombardments.

Successively occupied since 1790 by the District Council, a free secondary school, and by the Russians in 1814–1815, the buildings were handed over to the Grand Séminaire in 1822. Since the separation of the Church and State in 1905, they have been fitted up as a Museum.

The Museum was struck at the beginning of the bombardment on September 4, 1914, several pictures in the Modern Gallery being destroyed. Later, it was again hit by shells, but the greater part of the collections had already been removed to a place of safety.

THE OLD GRAND SÉMINAIRE (MUSEUM)

THE BED IN WHICH NAPOLEON SLEPT IN 1814

(In ruined house at No. 18 Rue de Vesle.)

Continue along the Rue Chanzy, which skirts the **Theatre** (1873), of which only the walls remain. *Take the Rue de Vesle (first street on the left. See Itinerary, p. 61).*

Among the ruins of this street, in the yard of No. 18 on the left, is a building of which only the ground-floor and front with large windows and spacious dormers remain.

It was there that Napoléon I. slept after his return to Rheims. His room had been preserved exactly as it was in 1814 (*see p.* 8).

At No. 27 are vestiges of the old **Hôtel Levesque de Pouilly.** Inside the court there was a 16th century house, the residence of a family which furnished Rheims with some remarkable administrators, chief among whom was *Levesque de Pouilly*, " lieutenant of the inhabitants." Among the celebrated guests received by him were Voltaire and Madame du Châtelet (1749).

THE PARIS GATE

THE VAULTING AND BELFRY OF THE CHURCH OF ST. JACQUES. (*Cliché LL.*)

In a letter to him, Lord Bolingbroke wrote : " *I know but three men who are worthy of governing the nation : You, Pope and myself.*"

On the right, between Nos. 44 *and* 46, *is the Rue St. Jacques.*

Follow the Rue de Vesle to the end, where the **Paris Gate** *stands, about* 1 *km. from the entrance to the Rue St. Jacques.*

This Gate replaced the Vesle Gate which formerly abutted on the river. In consequence of the growth of the city it was built in the *faubourg* about 1845. Its beautiful wrought-iron work (*photo opposite*), by the local master-locksmiths Lecoq and Revel, was erected by the City in 1774, at the time of the consecration of Louis XVI.

From the Paris Gate, return by the Rue de Vesle to the Rue St. Jacques, on the right of which stands the Church of St. Jacques.

The **Church of St. Jacques,** whose fine tower contributed to the charm of the general appearance of the city, was destroyed by the bombardments of 1918. Begun in the 12th century, it was finished in the 16th. Before the war, it was the only parish church in Rheims which had been preserved intact.

THE INTERIOR OF THE CHURCH OF ST. JACQUES. (*Cliché LL.*)

THE PLACE DROUET D'ERLON, BEFORE THE WAR

On the right: Belfry of the Church of St. Jacques.

The Rue St. Jacques leads to the long Place Drouet d'Erlon, which was much damaged by the bombardments of 1918 (*photo opposite*).

Formerly known as *Place de la Couture*, this square, like the old streets with picturesque names: *Rue des Telliers, Rue du Clou-dans-le-Fer, Rue de la Belle Image, Rue de la Grosse-Ecritoire, Rue du Cadran St. Pierre,* formed part of the *Quartier des Loges,* built in the 12th century by Cardinal Guillaume-aux-blanches-mains for the wood and iron workers. The house-fronts above the first storey rested mostly on wooden pillars, leaving recesses or covered galleries on the ground-floor.

In the centre of the square stood a statue of Marshal Drouet d'Erlon, afterwards removed to the crossing of the Boulevards Gerbert and Victor Hugo, and replaced by a **monumental fountain,** the gift of M. Subé.

Follow the Place Drouet d'Erlon to the Boulevard de la République, which skirts **The Promenades.**

THE PLACE DROUET D'ERLON, AFTER THE WAR

The Belfry of the Church of St. Jacques no longer exists.

THE SUBÉ FOUNTAIN, IN THE PLACE DROUET D'ERLON
Seen from the Rue Buirette (in ruins).

The Promenades, greatly damaged by the war, have sometimes been wrongly attributed to Le Nôtre. Their designer was a Rheims gardener, Jean le Roux Commenced in 1731, they were finished and extended in 1787. They were formerly reached by the Gates of Mars and Vesles, but preferably by the Promenade Gate specially opened in the ramparts in 1740 and inaugurated by Louis XV. in 1744, on his return from Flanders. The Promenades were first called *Cours Le Pelletier* (the name of the *Intendant of Champagne*, who approved the plans), then *Cours Royal*, after the passage of Louis XV. They were encroached upon by the railway station, built in 1860.

In the centre of the Promenades, opposite the station, in the *Square Colbert*, laid out by the landscape gardener Varé in 1860, is a statue of Colbert.

Take the Rue Thiers, which begins at the Square Colbert and leads to the **Hôtel-de-Ville.**

THE "SQUARE COLBERT" IN THE MIDDLE OF THE "PROMENADES"
The Entrance to the Station is just opposite this "Square."

THE TOWN HALL IN 1918

The Hôtel-de-Ville

This building, which was destroyed by shell-fire on May 13, 1917, was similar in many respects to the old Hôtel-de-Ville in Paris, burnt in 1871.

Commenced in 1627, from plans by the Rheims architect, Jean Bonhomme, it was completed in stages, at long intervals. Only the central *pavilion* and the left-hand portion were 17th century.

The building was a beautiful specimen of the architecture of the Louis XIII. period. Seventy-eight columns, Doric on the ground-floor and Corinthian on the first storey, framed the windows of the façade, whose bases on the first floor carried trophies in bas-relief and a graceful frieze. The niches in the central portico were empty, but the pediment on twisted columns enclose l an equestrian statue of Louis XIII.

In the interior, in the great vestibule, a staircase with a remarkable wrought-iron balustrade led to the City Library, which was destroyed by the fire of 1917 (*photo, p.* 73).

On the right, the room where the Municipal Council meetings were held, contained rich panelling alternated with paintings by Lamatte, commemorating episodes in the history of Rheims. On the left, the mayor's office contained magnificent Louis XVI. wood-work.

On the other side of the courtyard, in the centre of which is a statue of "La Vigne," by St. Marceaux, was the great marriage-hall, containing a Gallo-Roman mosaic, framed with rosettes and an interlaced border, representing a gladiatorial fight.

A number of the pictures and works of art in the Hôtel-de-Ville were saved by the firemen and soldiers. The mosaic in the marriage-hall was protected by sand-bags and is intact

In the Place de l'Hotel-de-Ville, between the Rue Thiers and the Banque de France, are two small streets : the Rue Salin and the Rue de Pouilly.

THE GRAND STAIRCASE OF THE TOWN HALL

At No. 5 of the Rue Salin, the old 17th century *Hôtel Coquebert*, which was destroyed by the shells, used to be the headquarters of the *Society of Friends of Old Rheims.* Several of the illustrations in this Guide are taken from the collections of this Society.

In the Rue de Pouilly, close to the Hôtel-de-Ville, are the **ruins** of the *Galeries Rémoises* stores. These shops were partly housed in a Gothic building, of which only a few chimney-stacks remain (*see chimney in photo below*).

Opposite the Hôtel-de-Ville take the Rue Colbert to the Place des Marchés.

THE RUE COLBERT, BETWEEN THE TOWN HALL AND THE MARKET-PLACE

RUINS IN THE MARKET-PLACE

Seen from the Rue de Tambour. The "Maison de l'Enfant d'Or" is among the ruined houses seen in the middle (see pp. 75 to 77). The "Hôtel de la Salle" and "Maison Fossier" (p. 76), on the right-hand side of the Square, are not visible in the above photograph.

The Place des Marchés

Built on the site of the ancient *forum*, the Market Square, before the war, still contained several remarkable 15th century wooden houses. Unfortunately, they were destroyed by the terrible bombardment of May 8–15, 1918, together with the Square.

THE "HOTEL DE LA SALLE"

On the left: the Carriage Entrance with Caryatids: Adam and Eve.

THE COURTYARD OF THE "HÔTEL DE LA SALLE"

The graceful Turret has partially collapsed.

After turning to the right, on leaving the Rue Colbert, and quite close to the Square, at No. 4 in the Rue de l'Arbalète, is the house, dating from the middle of the 16th century, where **J. B. de la Salle** was born.

Although this house suffered from the bombardments of 1918, its front is practically intact. It is the finest Renaissance front in Rheims, after that of **Le Vergeur's House** (*see p.* 85).

The carriage entrance is flanked with two life-size caryatids, popularly called *Adam and Eve*, on account of their nudity. Along the first storey runs a broad frieze ornamentated with trophies of arms and a shield of unknown significance. Between two windows of this storey a niche, resting on a console, is crowned with a canopy. The shops on the ground-floor somewhat spoilt the general look of the building. The interior of the house was less interesting than the front.

In the courtyard is a strikingly graceful three-storey turret (*photo above*), one side of which has collapsed.

Among the wooden houses destroyed by the bombardments of 1918 in the Place des Marchés, the following must be mentioned : the **Maison Fossier** (*see p.* 76), which stood in the Square at the right-hand corner of the Rue de l'Arbalète, and especially the **Maison de l'Enfant d'Or** (sometimes wrongly called the House of Jacques Callou), which stood near the Rue des Elus. The latter house took its name from an old sign representing the gilt figure of a sleeping child. Hence, punningly, the name *Golden* or *Sleeping* Child.

In spite of alterations, this house (*photo, p.* 77), with its pent-house roof, two overhanging storeys, windows crowned with finials, and sculptural decoration (*see carved console, p.* 77), was a well-preserved specimen of 15th century architecture.

From the Place des Marchés, follow the Rue Colbert to the **Place Royale.**

BEFORE THE WAR

See text, page 75.

AFTER THE WAR

THE "MAISON FOSSIER," BEFORE AND AFTER THE WAR

See Itinerary, p. 61 (No. 5 of *Explanatory Notes*).

SEE TEXT, P. 75

RUINS OF THE "MAISON DE L'ENFANT D'OR"

Second house on the left, after the Rue des Elus. (*See p.* 77.)

THIS VERY CURIOUS 15TH CENTURY HOUSE STOOD IN THE MARKET-PLACE

It was completely destroyed (*see p.* 76.)

THE "MAISON DE L'ENFANT D'OR," BEFORE THE WAR

BRACKET OF THE "MAISON DE L'ENFANT D'OR," REPRESENTING SAMSON SLAYING THE LION

THE PLACE ROYALE IN 1765

THE INAUGURATION OF THE STATUE OF "LOUIS LE BIENAIMÉ,"
August 26, 1765; engraving by Varin. The original statue (by Pigalle) is in the middle of the Square.

The Place Royale

The Place Royale, which had previously suffered severely on September 19–22, 1914, was completely destroyed by fire, with the exception of the modern buildings of the Société Générale Bank, during the bombardment of April 8–15, 1918.

Commenced in 1756, from plans by the architect Legendre, it formed an oblong, of severe and imposing appearance, at the cross-ways of the four main streets of the City. In order to carry out Legendre's plans, forty-nine houses had to be acquired and pulled down. The Square remained unfinished, only three of its sides being built. The Louis XV.–XVI. transition style houses were of uniform construction, and were remarkable for their arcades and eaveless roofs, around which latter ran a balustrade. The central house (formerly the *Hôtel des Fermes*) had a Doric front with a statue of

THE PLACE ROYALE IN 1918
The plinth of the statue was protected by masonry-work.

Mercury surrounded by children arranging bales or carrying grapes to the wine-press. A **statue of Louis XV.,** in the middle of the Square, was protected from the bombardments by masonry-work (*photos, p* 78 *and below*).

The monarch is represented in a Roman mantle and laurel wreath. On either side of the pedestal are two allegorical bronze figures. One, a woman, holding a helm with one hand and leading a lion with the other, symbolizes *gentleness of Government ;* the other, a contented man resting in the midst of abundance, represents *the happiness of nations.* The wolf and the lamb sleeping side by side at their feet are symbolical of the Golden Age.

The monument, inaugurated in 1765, is the work of Pigalle, but the two

STATUE OF LOUIS XV., PLACE ROYALE, WITH PARTIALLY BUILT PROTECTING WALL OF MASONRY

The two allegorical figures are supposed to be lik nesses the Sculptor Pigalle and his wife.

allegorical figures, which are supposed to be portraits of the sculptor and his wife, alone are original.

The original statue of Louis XV. was removed at the time of the Revolution (August 15, 1792), and sent to the foundry. It was first replaced by a pyramid surmounted by a "Fame," in memory of the defenders of the *Patrie*, then by a plaster Goddess of Liberty, and in 1803 by a trophy of arms and flags. The present statue, erected under Louis XVIII. (1818), is due to the sculptor Cartellier, and is an exact replica of the original one.

It was on the steps of the monument that the Conventionist Ruhl smashed the Sacred Ampulla under the Revolution.

From the Place Royale, return to the Market Square, cross over to the Rue de Tambour (parallel with the Rue Colbert).

The Rue de Tambour owes its name either to the statue of a tambourine-player on one of its houses, or to the presence of the town-drummer who lived in it. It was first damaged, then burnt, in April, 1918.

THE STATUES OF THE MUSICIANS' HOUSE

The house was destroyed by bombardment, but the statues were saved.

Previous to 1918, old houses in this street were still numerous. The most celebrated was the now completely destroyed **Musicians' House** (*photo above*), the true origin of which is unknown.

It has variously been supposed to have been the house of a rich burgess, of the Tom Fiddlers' Brotherhood, and the Mint of the Archbishops of Rheims. The first storey of the façade had been preserved intact since the 13th century. In the Gothic niches which separated the mullioned and transomed windows, five large seated figures on carved consoles (*photo above*) represented *a tambourine and flute player, a piper, a falconer* with crossed legs, *a harpist* and *an organ-grinder* crowned with a garland of flowers. The falcon on the wrist of the central figure was removed by the organisers of the consecration of Charles X., as it was feared that the royal banners might get caught on it.

Fortunately, these statues, which are remarkable for their natural expression and vigour. were removed to a place of safety before the house was destroyed.

Thanks to a public subscription, the town was able to acquire them shortly before the war, thus preventing them from being sold abroad.

The cellars of this house are curious, but there exists no proof that they date back, as has been said, to the Roman period.

The adjoining house (No. 22) is 14th century, and probably dates back

14TH CENTURY DOORWAY, 22 RUE DE TAMBOUR

to about the end of the reign of Philippe-le-Bel. Its front has been greatly spoilt, but still contains a fine door surmounted by an elliptical arch (*photo above*).

At No. 13 of this street, two 13th century carved heads, one of a man and the other of a woman wearing one of the mortar-shaped hats in fashion until the end of the reign of St. Louis, have been built into the façade.

At the end of the Rue de Tambour, take the Rue de Mars, on the right of the Hôtel-de-Ville, at the end of which, on the left, stands the Triumphal Arch of the **Mars Gate.**

THE RUE DE MARS. THE TOWN HALL IS ON THE LEFT

MARS GATE

The Mars Gate

This monument was long believed to be a Roman **gate**—hence its name—although the ornamentation of its four sides proves that it cannot originally have been connected with the ramparts. It was only in the Middle Ages that it was included in the fortified castle (*photo, p.* 6) built by the archbishops a few steps to the rear. About 1334 its arcades were walled up, while towards 1554 it was buried under a mass of rubbish during the building of the fortifications. Partly disinterred in 1594, when the archbishops' castle was pulled down, it was not completely cleared until 1816–1817 Restored, then classed as an *historical monument* (thanks to Prosper Mérimée), it is one of the largest Roman structures remaining in France. Forty-four feet high, one hundred and eight wide, and sixteen thick, it was really a triumphal arch built on the Cæsarean Way at the entrance to the town,

18TH CENTURY ENGRAVING BY COLLIN OF THE VAULTING OF THE ROMULUS AND REMUS ARCADE OF THE MARS GATE

In the centre: Romulus and Remus suckled by the she-wolf.

probably in the 4th century. It comprises three arches separated by fluted Corinthian columns which support the entablature. On the two main façades between the columns are carved medallions and niches which have lost their statues. The vaulting of the arches is divided into sunken panels, the carving of which is mostly in a good state of preservation. Under the eastern arch *Romulus and Remus* are seen suckled by the she-wolf. Under the middle arch, the twelve months of the year, represented by persons (five of whom have been destroyed), occupied in the labours of the four seasons, surround Abundance and Fortune. Under the western arch Love is seen descending from the sky above Leda and the Swan.

Behind the Mars Gate is the Place de la République, containing a statue by Bartholdi, damaged by shell-fire. *In front of the Gate, take the Rue*

HÔTEL NOËL DE MUIRE

Note the curious masonry-work of the first storey, composed of polygonal stones in relief.

Henri IV., leading behind the Hôtel-de-Ville, then turn to the left into the Rue de Sedan. The house at No. 3 was destroyed by shells, except the **Louis XVI. front** with its gracefully carved garlands, which escaped injury.

Take the Rue du Grenier-à-Sel, on the right, to the **Hôtel Noël de Muire,** *on the left, at the corner of the Rue Linguet.*

This house consists of the remains of a sort of Henry II. manor with turrets and dormer-windows. The walls, rounded at the corners like those of the Templars, are of brick and dressed stone. The plinth separating the two stories is decorated with carved wreathed foliage. Fret-work and hexagonal points frame the windows, while a broad cornice on consoles carries the roof. Formerly the residence of the lords of Muire, this house was popularly known as the *Maison des Petits Pâtés,* on account of the polygonal shape of the stones in relief. Theodore de Bèze, one of the leaders of the Reformation in France, lived there with his friend, Noël de Muire.

THE RUE DU MARC

Take the Rue du Marc, which continues the Rue du Grenier-à-Sel (photo above).

The **Rue du Marc** was the quarter where the old noble families and the higher *bourgeoisie* of Rheims lived. It suffered considerably from the bombardments.

At No. 3 is a Henry IV. house, the windows of which are framed with graceful ornamentation (*photo below*).

However, the most remarkable house in the street is undoubtedly the **Hôtel Nicolas le Vergeur** (No. 1), which, unfortunately, was partly destroyed by the shells (*see p.* 85).

HOUSE DATING BACK TO THE REIGN OF HENRI IV. (1589-1610) AT NO. 3 RUE DU MARC

The Hôtel Nicolas Le Vergeur

The interior building, which has a 17th century carriage entrance, offers two fine examples of 15th and 16th century architecture. It is the finest Renaissance structure in Rheims. The main front, incomparably the most graceful, was but little damaged by the bombardments (*photo below*).

On the ground-floor the great arched doorway is divided by a wooden post into two delicately carved compartments. Pilasters decorated with heads, flowers, birds, and horns of plenty frame the three stone-mullioned windows. Above these runs a frieze of trophies and medallions, with portraits of noble lords with upturned moustaches and pointed beards, and of great ladies with *collerettes* and high head-dresses, gracious or haughty, standing well out in relief.

On the first storey, carved panels above the windows form a sort of broad frieze of bas-reliefs representing men-at-arms or knights of the time of

HÔTEL NICOLAS LE VERGEUR

François I. and Henri II. fighting at tournaments with lance, sword, or pike.

In one of the rooms overlooking the Rue Pluche were, a fine stone *mantel-piece* decorated with graceful delicate foliage; a timberwork *ceiling* with large and small beams, carrying panels decorated with scrolls, and 15th century *tile-flooring* of terra-cotta, varnished and painted green and yellow.

At the back of the courtyard, a building, supposed by some to be an old chapel, had been transformed into vast cellars and store-rooms. The *oaken ceiling* of the latter, about fifty feet long and twenty-one broad, destroyed in 1918, was one of the most beautiful in the world. The beams, whose extremities carried grotesque figures, were carved on all their sides with foliage, dragons, birds, and fruits. The beams were connected by joists resting on stems, which represented apes, dragons, persons, and foliage. Between the joists the panels had the appearance of scrolls.

After visiting the Hôtel Le Vergeur, turn to the right into the Rue Pluche, which leads to the Place des Marchés. Skirt the Square on the left, then take the first street on the left: **Rue Courmeaux.**

HÔTEL ROGIER DE MONCLIN, 18 RUE COURMEAUX

At No. 18 *are the* ruins of the **Hôtel Rogier de Monclin,** destroyed after April, 1918. This house dated back to the Louis XV. period, but had been disfigured by modern alterations. The façade overlooking the courtyard, the entrance-hall, and the staircase with ornamental balustrade, were interesting. At the time of the consecration of Louis XVI., one of the saloons was furnished for the King's brother, the Comte (or *Monsieur*) d'Artois, whence the name "*Rue de Monsieur,*" formerly borne by the Rue Courmeaux.

At No. 30 is a Renaissance door, almost intact (*photo below*). *At No.* 34, *at the corner of the Rue Legendre,* is a late 16th century house, whose interior arrangement and façade are intact, except for the woodwork of the windows, which was modernised in the 18th century. It

RENAISSANCE DOOR,
30, *Rue Courmeaux.*

CÉRÈS ESPLANADE

was built on the site of the old wool-market, after Marshal de Saint-Paul, at the time of the League, had compelled the inhabitants of the Faubourg Cérès to destroy their houses.

Return to the Rue Courmeaux and take the Rue Bonhomme on the left, which leads to the Rue Cérès.

The **Rue Cérès** was totally destroyed by fire, from the Place Royale to the Post Office, which had to be given up in the autumn of 1914.

At No. 30 is the **Chamber of Commerce,** one of the finest late 18th century buildings in Rheims. The magnificent Louis XVI. rooms escaped practically uninjured. The staircase leading to the first storey, with its delicate balustrade, is very remarkable.

CHURCH OF ST. ANDRÉ,
Rue du Faubourg Cérès.

INTERIOR OF THE CHURCH OF ST. ANDRÉ

The Rue Cérès ends at the Esplanade Cérès (*photo, p.* 87), which was made outside the old ramparts near the Cérès Gate. The name Cérès is derived from a tower that long served as a prison (*carcer*, whence by corruption *chair, cère*, and then by false mythological association, *Cérès*). It was in this tower (no longer existing, but famous as early as the 9th century) that, according to the *chansons de geste*, Ogier the Dane, handed over by Charlemagne to the custody of the Bishop of Rheims, was incarcerated.

RELIQUARY OF ST. ANDRÉ

From the Esplanade continue, if desired, by the Rue du Faubourg Cérès (greatly damaged by the bombardments), to the **Church of St. André,** a modern building erected by the architect Brunette.

It was struck several times by shells and will have to be rebuilt. As early as the first bombardment of September 4th, 1914, shell splinters damaged the doorway, transept, stained glass (part of which was 16th century and came from the old church), small organ, and the painting of the *Baptism of Clovis*. Subsequently, the vaulting and parts of the walls collapsed.

The Church possesses a precious **reliquary** of copper (15th century) and a **statue of St. André** (patron of the church) of painted and gilded stone, attributed without authority, to Pierre Jacques.

HÔTEL THIRET DE PRAIN IN 1916
19, *Rue Eugène Desteuque.*

Return to the Esplanade Cérès, turn to the left at the beginning of the Boulevard de la Paix, then to the right into the **Rue Eugène Desteuque.**
At No. 19 *of this street* are the ruins of the **Hôtel Thiret de Prain.**

The Hôtel Thiret de Prain

This was a mansion in the days of Henry IV. and Louis XIII. Richelieu stayed there in 1641.

An imposing building, bordered with streets on its four sides, it had retained its original appearance. The carriage-entrance in the Rue Eugène-Desteuque alone had been rebuilt in 1697. The principal entrance was surmounted with a gallery, the walls, ceiling and beams of which were covered with delicate decorative paintings.

On the first floor one of the corner rooms, looking east, contained a large

HÔTEL THIRET DE PRAIN IN 1918
These two photographs illustrate the systematic destructions practised by the Germans.

INTERIOR FAÇADE OF THE CLOISTER OF THE FRANCISCAN FRIARS
In the courtyard of No. 9, Rue des Trois-Raisinets.

Henry IV. mantelpiece, above which were the arms of the nobles of Prain. Only the metallic portion remains.

The dove-cot of the Hôtel, a massive square tower with pent-house roof, overlooking the Rue d'Avenay, was destroyed by the bombardments.

On the left of the Rue Eugène-Desteuque, opposite the Hôtel Thiret-de-Prain, is the Rue des Trois-Raisinets. At No. 9 are the ruins of a Franciscan Cloister (*photo above*).

This street (*photo below*), like the Cloister, suffered severely from the bombardments.

Return to the Rue Eugène-Desteuque and follow the same as far as the Rue de la Grue (*on the right*). This street was badly damaged by shell-fire and is impracticable for motor-cars.

It was named after the sign carved on a stone (*photo, p.* 91) of the house at No. 5 (entirely destroyed by the shells). At the end stood the house where

RUINS OF THE MARGOTIN FACTORY
14, *Rue des Trois-Raisinets.*

THE SIGN WHICH GAVE ITS NAME TO THE RUE DE LA GRUE

It was at No. 5, but has been destroyed.

J. B. Colbert was born (at the corner of the Rues Cérès and de Nanteuil, *photo below*).

Return to the Rue Eugène-Desteuque, follow it as far as the Rue de l'Université. *Turn into the latter on the left.*

This street was destroyed as early as September, 1914. At No. 25 are the ruins of a Professional School for Girls, formerly the St. Martha Hospital. The latter, also known as the "Hôpital des Magneuses," was founded in the 17th century by Mesdames de Magneux, and rebuilt in the 18th century in the Louis XVI. style.

RUINS OF THE HOUSE WHERE COLBERT WAS BORN

At the corner of the Rues Cérès and de Nanteuil.

At No. 40, opposite the Sub-Prefecture, now in ruins, is the **Maison de Jean Maillefer,** named after the rich merchant who built it in 1652. It was scarcely finished, when it was chosen—and this was a source of pride to its owner—as an abode for Anne of Austria, at the time of the consecration of Louis XIV. The inside of the courtyard alone has retained practically its ancient appearance. The front looking on the street had recently been put back and altered. Some of the sculpture which adorned it came from another house.

A short distance farther on, on the left, is the Place Godinot, named after a canon of the 18th century, who caused numerous alterations to be made in the decoration of the choir and sanctuary of the Cathedral.

Take the Rue St. Just on the right, and follow its continuation (the Rue des Anglais) as far as the Rue d'Anjou, *which take on the right.*

The **Hôtel de la Pourcelette** (No. 7) evokes memories of *Mabillon,* who lived there when a young student at the University of Rheims.

At the end of the Rue d'Anjou, turn to the left into the Rue du Cardinal de Lorraine, and follow the same to the short Rue des Tournelles *on the left.*

In the house at No. 3 of this street were incorporated the turret and two principal windows of an old Gothic 16th century structure, situated at No. 18 of the Rue des Anglais, and in ruins since 1898. The drawing-room likewise contains a large stone chimney-piece, which formerly stood in the great hall of the old house.

At the end of the Rue des Tournelles, turn to the right into the Rue des Fusiliers, which leads to the Place du Parvis. Cross the latter to the Rue Tronson Ducoudray. Follow this street, which runs between the Palais de Justice *and*

LOUIS XIII. DOOR

At No. 20 Rue du Carrouge.

the Theatre, *turn to the left, in front of the latter, into the Rue de Vesle, and take the first street on the right,* the Rue de Talleyrand.

Follow this street, the greater part of which was destroyed by fire during the bombardments of April, 1918. It suffered further damage in the months that followed, and a number of interesting old houses were destroyed.

Turn into the first street on the right (Rue du Cadran St. Pierre), and follow the same as far as the Rue de la Clef. Take the latter on the right.

Before doing so, however, take a look at the **fine Louis XIII. entrance** (*photo, p.* 92) of the house at No. 20 of the Rue du Carrouge opposite.

At No. 4 *of the Rue de la Clef are the* ruins of the former **Hôtel de Bezannes,** partly built by Pierre de Bezannes, Lieutenant of Rheims in 1458 This house contains some fine 16th and 18th century woodwork.

The Rue des Deux Anges, which continues the Rue de la Clef, leads to the

RUE CARNOT

The Place Royale is seen in the background.

Place du Palais, destroyed during the bombardments of April, 1918. *In this square stands the* **Palais de Justice.** The *Palais* replaced the old Hôtel-Dieu, but has been almost entirely rebuilt. It is a building of little note, the principal entrance in particular being stiff to excess.

Its only interest is provided by two relics of the past: the vast cellars or subterranean vaults with pointed arches supported by columns with Gothic capitals; and the façade of the Audience-Chamber, formerly the principal ward of the old Hôtel Dieu, the exterior of which has retained its venerable appearance and the interior, vestiges of its lofty timber-work and wainscoted vaulting.

The ground-floor of the *Palais* alone escaped damage from fire and the shells, thanks to a terrace of reinforced concrete.

On the left of the Palais take the Rue Carnot, destroyed by the bombardments of April, 1918.

The Rue Carnot communicates with the courtyard of the Chapter-House, also burnt, by a great gate and passage which pass right through a house.

This entrance was built about 1530, in the transition style between the Gothic and Renaissance. Its elliptical arch bears a scutcheon with the arms of the Chapter. Consoles, decorated with grotesque figures, support the beams. The points of the turrets have disappeared, a supporting shaft has been mutilated, and the carved wooden leaves of the door have been removed to the Lycée, yet the gate is still imposing.

It is the last remaining vestige of the Chapter buildings which, with their gates closing at the same time as those of the city, at the sound of the bell, formed a " city within a city." In point of fact, the Chapter was once lord of that part of the city which lies around the Cathedral, and which it adminis-

DOOR OF THE CHAPTER-HOUSE COURTYARD

The Northern Transept of the Cathedral is seen in the background.

tered. The canons, jealous of their prerogatives, were often in conflict with the archbishops.

A few capitals and shafts of the ancient cloister of the Chapter, adjoining the Cathedral, were recently discovered and placed under one of the pent-houses built between the buttresses of Notre-Dame.

Go through the gate, cross the Place du Chapitre, follow the Rue du Préau towards the Cathedral, then turn to the right into the Rue Robert de Coucy, which leads back to the Place du Parvis Notre-Dame

SECOND ITINERARY FOR VISITING RHEIMS

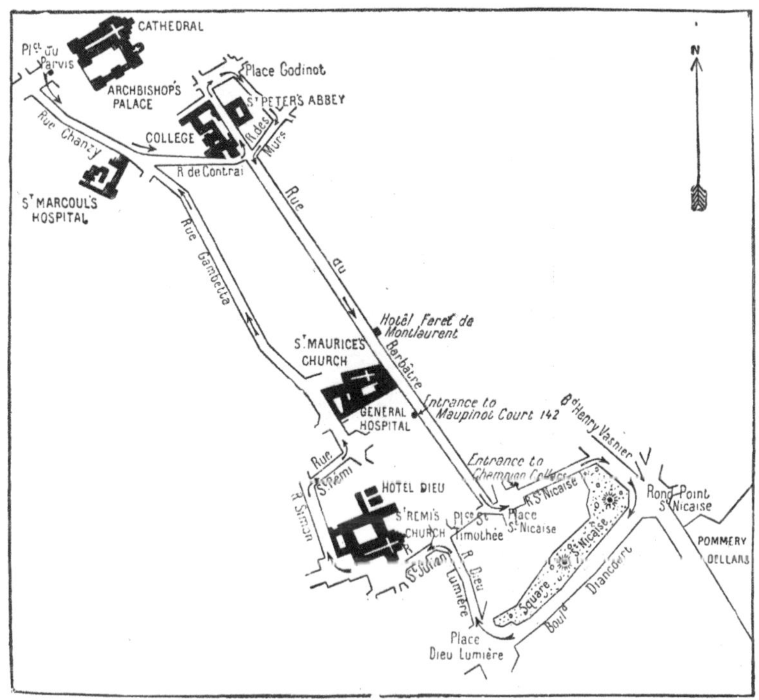

Starting from the Place du Parvis-Notre-Dame, take the Rue Libergier, opposite the Cathedral. Turn to the left into the Rue Chanzy, which was destroyed by the bombardments of April–August, 1918.

RUE CHANZY

DOOR AND BALCONY OF THE HÔTEL DE COURTAGNON, (*18th Century*), *at No.* 71 *Rue Chanzy*

The ruins of the 18th century **Hôtel Lagoille de Courtagnon** may be seen at No. 71 of this street. It was destroyed by the bombardments of April, 1918, with the exception of a part of the front. The finely carved door and remarkable ironwork of the balcony are visible in the above photograph.

ORNAMENTAL RAIN-WATER PIPE-HEAD OF LEAD UNDER THE ROOF OF THE HOSPICE NOËL CAQUÉ (*see p.* 97)

GALLO-ROMAN BAS-RELIEF *at No. 65, Rue de l'Université. This bas-relief and the one opposite, on the wall of the Lycée, are the last remaining vestiges of a Gallo-Roman gate.*

The **Hospice Noël Caqué** (formerly Hospice St. Marcoul), *on the right*, was seriously damaged by the bombardments of April, 1918. It dated from the middle of the 17th century, and was well preserved, with the exception of the chapel, rebuilt in 1873.

Take the Rue de Contrai, on the left, which leads to the Rue de l'Université. Inserted in the façade of the house at No. 65 (*on the right*), and in the wall of the Lycée (*on the left*), are two stone **bas-reliefs** ornamented with trophies of arms and Roman insignia, the sole remaining vestiges of the *Porte Basée* (*from Basilea*) which formerly stood there on the Cæsarean way, at the southern extremity of the Gallo-Roman town. (*See photo above of the right-hand bas-relief.*)

Follow the Rue de l'Université and skirt the **Lycée de Garçons,** of which

THE FAÇADE OF THE LYCÉE, DESTROYED BY THE BOMBARDMENTS

DOOR OF THE PETIT LYCÉE, 5, *Rue Vauthier-le-Noir. On either side of the arcade are heads of "Jean qui rit" and "Jean qui pleure."*

only the chapel and one of the buildings are left. The rest was burnt or destroyed by shell-fire.

The Lycée replaced the old *Collège des Bons Enfants*, founded in the Middle Ages, and rebuilt in the 16th century by the Cardinal de Lorraine, founder of the University of Rheims.

Of the old *Collège*, only the central part remained, in the second court built by Archbishop Charles Maurice Le Tellier in 1686 and the following years.

The gate of the *Cour des Etudes* dates from 1688.

The ancient door of the Collège—the tympana of whose arcading contain two laughing and crying heads—was transferred to the entrance of the *Petit Lycée*, at No. 5 of the street on the right of the Lycée (Rue Vauthier-le-Noir) (*photo above*).

Shortly after the Lycée, turn to the right into the Place Godinot, then take the Rue St. Pierre-les-Dames on the right. At No. 8 are the ruins of the **Abbey of St. Pierre-les-Dames.**

Of this celebrated Abbey, where several royal persons stayed: *Mary Stuart* twice, in her childhood and after she was widowed; *Henry IV.*, on a visit to his cousin, the Abbess Renée II.; *Anne of Austria*, of whom the *Congrégation* library contains a portrait; there remains hardly anything but two 16th century *pavillons* belonging to the period when Renée de Lorraine, sister of the Queen of Scotland and aunt of Mary Stuart, was abbess of the convent. Built of stone and brick with marble incrustations, and adorned with beautiful carvings, these *pavillons* were pure Renaissance in style. The head of an angel with unfolded wings and the head of a grinning demon surmounted the two windows of one of the ground-floors. On the first floor of the same *pavillon* the window, framed with delicate ornaments, opened above a cornice, the principal sculptural subject of which was a nude woman, helmeted, suckling two children.

RUINS OF THE ABBEY OF ST. PIERRE-LES-DAMES, 8, *Rue St. Pierre-les-Dames*

The Rue St. Pierre-les-Dames leads to the Rue des Murs, into which turn to the right, then to the left into the Rue du Barbâtre. Follow the latter to the end. This street suffered greatly from the early bombardments, and was almost entirely destroyed in the summer of 1918.

At Nos. 137 *and* 139, *at the corner of the Rue Montlaurent,* are the ruins of the **Hôtel Féret de Montlaurent.**

Hôtel Féret de Montlaurent.

This large building, occupied by the *Cercle Catholique,* was commenced about 1540 by Hubert Féret, a *Lieutenant* of the people, and the most

GALLERY FACING THE COURTYARD OF THE HÔTEL FÉRET DE MONTLAURENT

The statues in the niches represent the sun and planets.

celebrated member of a family which played an important part at Rheims in the 15th, 16th, and 17th centuries. The outside façade has been greatly altered. At No. 137 it was entirely rebuilt under Louis XVI. At No. 139 the ground-floor openings have been modified.

As in many of the mansions of the 16th century, most of the decoration is on the inner façades. Inside the courtyard, on the ground-floor of the wing abutting on the Rue Montlaurent, there is a six-arched gallery which was damaged but not destroyed (*photo*, p. 99). Between the arch-centres and at the ends of the gallery are seven niches, three feet high, enclosing stone statues of the sun and the six planets known in the 16th century.

Taken in their order they are: **Saturn,** with a scythe in his hand and serpent round his arm, devouring a child, and the zodiacal signs Aquarius and Capricornus at his feet; **Jupiter,** holding a lighted torch, with Sagittarius at his feet; **Mars,** armed from head to foot, surmounting Cancer and Aries; the **Sun,** personified by Phœbus with flowing mantle, a lion at his side; **Venus,** clothed only in her hair, surmounting Taurus and Balœna; **Mercury,** with wings on his head and heels, the caduceus in his hand, Virgo and Gemini at his feet; the **Moon,** represented by Diana bearing a crescent; below her Scorpio.

The escutcheons on the wall at the back of this façade bear the initials of Régnault Féret, who completed the mansion. In the second court there are still vestiges of the chapel of this family.

At No. 142 *of the same street,* the entrance to the **Cour Maupinot** (one of the numerous *cours* which have survived in Rheims) is framed in pilasters, the carved entablature of which supports a triangular pediment (*photo below*).

The Rue Barbâtre is continued by the Rue des Salines, which leads to the Place St. Nicaise.

ENTRANCE TO MAUPINOT COURT. THE DOORWAY IS RENAISSANCE, 142, *Rue du Barbâtre.* *See Itinerary, p.* 95

The Place St. Nicaise was destroyed by the bombardments of April–August, 1918. It took its name from the celebrated Bishop of Rheims, who, with his sister St. Eutropia, was put to death by the Vandals in 407.

The Church of St. Nicaise, rebuilt in the 13th century by Libergier and Robert de Coucy, was destroyed at the time of the Revolution. Amongst other curiosities it contained a loose pillar, which Peter the Great had pointed out to him at the time of his journey through Rheims.

At the corner of the Place St. Nicaise, between the Boulevard Victor-Hugo and the Rue St. Nicaise, is the entrance to the **Champion Cellars,** in which the *Dubail* school was installed during the war (*see p.* 24).

Take the Rue St. Nicaise to the Boulevard Henry Vasnier (photo below), turn into the latter, on the right, and follow same as far as the **Rond-Point St. Nicaise.**

All this part of the town, which was quite close to the German lines, was constantly under the fire of their guns. It was violently bombarded during the German offensives of May, June and July, 1918.

Near the Rond-Point de St. Nicaise are the **Pommery Cellars,** which gave shelter to many citizens and school-classes during the war (*see p.* 24).

The Pommery Cellars

These cellars are among the finest in Rheims, and form, with their eleven miles of streets, squares and boulevards lighted by electricity, rail-tracks, waggons, lifts, electric pumps and siphons, quite an underground city. A visit to them will give the tourist an idea of the importance and complexity of the Champagne wine industry in Rheims.

THE "HENRY VASNIER," SEEN FROM THE "ROND-POINT ST. NICAISE"

TRENCHES AND SHELTERS IN THE SQUARE ST. NICAISE

See Itinerary, p. 95, and panorama seen from the top of St. Nicaise Hill, p. 27.

The Boulevard Diancourt, which skirts the Square St. Nicaise, begins at the Rond-Point St. Nicaise.

This square was much cut up by the bombardments, and by the trenches and defensive works made there during the war (*photo above*).

The square contains two eminences, from the top of which there is a fine panoramic view of Rheims.

The photograph on page 27 was taken from the eminence nearest the Rond-Point St. Nicaise.

The other eminence is crowned by a limestone tower—all that remains of the ancient city ramparts.

Follow the Boulevard Diancourt to the Place Dieu-Lumière.

The name *Dieu-Lumière*, borne by the old gate through which Joan-of-Arc and the Dauphin entered Rheims, was not derived, as supposed at the Renaissance, from the Sun-God Apollo, but from the old Gate *Dieu-li-Mire* (God the Physician), so called in the Middle Ages on account of the proximity of a Cistercian hospital.

Cross the square and take the Rue Dieu-Lumière on the right to the Place St.-Timothée. The wood-panelled houses, whose *loges* faced the Place St.-Timothée, were destroyed by the bombardments of April–September, 1918, except the one at the corner of the Rue St. Julien. This house, though severely damaged, has retained its butcher's stall with 17th century wooden balustrading.

Take the Rue St. Julien on the left to the Place St.-Remi, in which stands the **Church of St. Remi.**

The Church of St. Remi

The Church of St. Remi is the oldest church in Rheims, and one of the oldest in all France. Although it is not certain that it replaced a Roman basilica, said to have stood on the site of the present transept, there is no doubt that Gallo-Roman building materials, taken from neighbouring edifices, were used in its construction or restoration.

To-day, the church covers a ground-space of about an acre and a quarter. In shape a Latin cross, it measures inside about 450 feet in length, 98 feet in breadth and 124 feet in height under the vaulting. Only the southern façade shows to advantage, but in spite of its varied styles, which mark the different stages of its growth, the church realises to the full the purpose of its founders. Its architecture and decoration, especially in the interior, make it, as was intended, a grand and dignified depository for sacred remains.

The Church of St. Remi stands on the site of a former cemetery, in the middle of which was the Chapel of St. Christopher, where St. Remi was buried. The chapel soon became popular and grew rapidly, especially between the 6th and 9th centuries, when it became a great fortified church. The present church, which replaced it, is not only one of the finest Romanesque churches in the north of France, but also forms a curious epitome of the history of architecture for several centuries. Begun in 1039 under Abbot Thierry, it was still far from finished when consecrated in 1049 by Pope Leo IX. Building was continued in 1170 by Abbot Pierre de Celle, the future Bishop of Chartres, whose restorations were the first application of the Gothic style to a great building in Rheims; in the 13th and 14th centuries, under Abbot Jean Canart, and in the 15th century, under Abbot Robert de Lenoncourt. Partially transformed at the end of the 16th century, it has been restored and partly rebuilt at intervals since 1839.

The Church of St. Remi during the War

The Church of St. Remi escaped severe damage until the middle of 1918. The bombardment of September 4, 1914, injured one of the tapestries depicting the life of St. Remi, and destroyed a fine painting: *The Entry of Clovis into Rheims*. The bombardment of November 16, 1914, wrecked the apsidal chapel of the Virgin, bringing down the vaulting, destroying the key-stone and pointed arches, crushing the altar beneath a heap of ruins, smashing the magnificent windows of the apsidal gallery, and destroying the priceless 12th century stained-glass depicting *Christ crucified between the Virgin and St. John*. The Church narrowly escaped destruction when the Hôtel-Dieu Hospital was burnt down in 1916. From April, 1918, it was marked down by the German batteries. The roof was entirely burnt, and the dummy vaulting of the nave collapsed. Of the fine 15th century timber-work nothing remains, but parts of the lofty 13th century vaulting over the choir and transept withstood the bombardment. The treasure, tapestries, sacristy doors, storied tile-flooring of the chapel of St. Eloi, the old stained-glass of the lofty windows, and the apsidal windows round the gallery of the first storey, were saved by the Historical Monuments Department.

The tomb of St. Remi is intact. The relics of the saint which, at the request of the Archbishop of Rheims had not been disturbed, were removed by the vicar of the parish at the time of the final evacuation of the town. The reliquary was taken away by officers at a later date, while the church was burning.

The Apse of St. Remi Church

The Apse was rebuilt under Pierre de Celle in 1170, in early Gothic. Five three-sided radiating chapels arranged in three stages, one behind the other, have flowing and elegant lines, broken by the enormous projections of the buttresses which were added at a later period.

This apse is one of the earliest religious edifices in France, in which flying buttresses were employed.

The latter, very simple in design, rest on outside fluted columns detached from the wall of the apse. This is one of the last examples of fluting, as applied to columns, the process disappearing generally with the introduction of pointed architecture, only to reappear at the Renaissance.

The persistence of this fluting is doubtless explained by the influence of the many specimens of Roman architecture which Rheims had preserved

The Doorway of the Southern Transept

Although the transept dates from the 11th century, its southern façade was built in 1480 by Robert de Lenoncourt.

The doorway, which bears the Lenoncourt arms, comprises only one door, divided by a pillar with statues of St. Remi and the Virgin.

The deep vaulting of the door is ornamented with vine-foliage. At the base, in the supporting walls, are statues of St. Sixtus and St. Sinicius (the first missionaries to Rheims) bare-footed, clothed in long embroidered mantles and holding books. In the vaulting above the head-covering of the missionaries are eight groups of statuettes representing episodes in the Life and Passion of Jesus.

Tourists who follow the Itinerary on page 95, come out by the Rue St. Julien, in front of the doorway of the south transept. The latter is between the ruined apse (*on the right*) and the south lateral façade (*on the left*).

SOUTHERN TRANSEPT OF ST. REMI CHURCH

DOORWAY OF THE SOUTHERN TRANSEPT (*see photo, p.* 104)

The 15th century leaves of the door are composed of wood panels in blind arcading, ornamented with flowering clover.

On the buttresses which frame the doorway are five statues of saints, including St. Remi, St. Benedict, and St. Christopher carrying a kneeling Jesus on his shoulder.

The tympanum of the gable above the great flamboyant window is arranged on a Gothic pediment. Its decoration represents the *Assumption of the Virgin and her crowning in Heaven.*

On the top of the pediment, and crowning the whole, is St. Michael trampling Satan underfoot.

The whole of the doorway is a beautiful example of Flamboyant Gothic. Its rich carvings and delicate ornamentation are in striking contrast with the severity of the rest of the building.

At the intersection of the transept, there was formerly a wooden spire, built in 1394, which was pulled down as unsafe in 1825, by order of those who had charge of the arrangements connected with the consecration of Charles X.

On the right-hand side of the transept, and also in the north transept, are small semi-circular chapels.

South Lateral Façade

This front has the bare, massive appearance of the 11th century buildings. The remarkable Roman arches, massive buttresses and blind doorway, framed by two primitive capitals with a wreath-shaped astragal, are apparently vestiges of constructions of an earlier date than those of Abbot Thierry.

The semi-cylindrical abutments are among the oldest of mediæval buttresses. They are crowned with cones or capitals, the greater part of which are devoid of decoration.

The West Front of St. Remi Church

Between its two towers, this gabled façade, the recesses and blind arcading of which form almost its sole decoration, is in strong contrast with the principal façade of the Cathedral. At once elegant and severe, like most of the monastic buildings of the 12th century, it lacks unity. All that part situated above the five windows of the first storey, including the rose-window, has been rebuilt in modern times. The very simple rose-window, between two lines of superimposed arcading, is protected, in the Champagne style, by a relieving-arch. The northern tower (*on the left*) was almost entirely rebuilt in the 19th century, on the lines of the old one. The simpler southern tower (*on the right*), with its arched windows and loopholes, is Roman of the 11th or 12th century. The pointed part of the façade is late 12th century, and dates from the time of the restorations by Pierre de Celle.

Three doors open on the nave. The central one is flanked by two columns with statues of St. Peter and St. Remi. The marble and granite columns came, no doubt, from some neighbouring Gallo-Roman building. These statues, with arms pressed close to their sides in the ancient stiff manner, are probably from the original basilicas.

THE NAVE (*seen from the Choir*) (*Cliché LL.*)

The Inner Side of the Western Doorway

Here, the architecture is peculiar. Pierced columns form a gallery connecting the upper courses. The galleries of the first storey are supported by two great columnar shafts, each formed of two portions joined by a stone ring and surmounted by bell-shaped marble capitals. The columns and capitals are Gallo-Roman.

The Nave

Alterations were made at different times to the nave which, in the 11th century, had a timber-work roof. Pierre de Celle lengthened it by two bays, the pointed arches of which contrast with the circular ones of the lower bays, and also increased its height. *Note the ogives above the round arches.* The visible timber-work was replaced with vaulting on diagonal ribs sustained by clusters of small Gothic columns backing up against the Roman piers, the latter being still visible. These heavy piers (composed of fourteen small columns) which surround the central nave, and whose capitals (*photo, p.* 108), with Barbaric wreathed astragals and foliage, recall the Carolingian period, contrast strikingly with the lightness of the apse. They are undoubtedly 11th century. All the stone vaulting of the nave, as far as the transept,

ROMAN CAPITAL IN THE NAVE

was replaced after 1839 with wood and plaster, which collapsed under the bombardments of 1918, when the roof was burnt.

The pulpit, with its Benedictine monogram, is late 17th century. It is

THE NAVE AND CHOIR IN 1914 (*Cliché LL.*)

TRIFORIUM OF ST. REMI CHURCH (*seen from entrance*)

ornamented with three bas-reliefs : *St. Remi receiving the Sacred Ampulla, St. Benedict imploring the Holy Spirit,* and *St. Benedict giving the Injunction to his monks.* As far as the pulpit, on both sides of the nave, the granite columns resting on the piers date from the Gallo-Roman period.

The side-aisles of the nave are surmounted with a triforium (*photo above*) with semi-circular vaulting at right-angles to the nave. The south aisle is almost entirely in ruins (*photo, p.* 107).

THE NAVE AND CHOIR IN 1919

The Tapestries

The priceless tapestries which, before the war, decorated the tribunals of the side-aisles, were saved.

Those given by Robert de Lenoncourt and restored by *Les Gobelins*, are rich in composition and decorative effect. In an architectural frame of the Renaissance period, they represent the following legendary scenes from the life of St. Remi, the costumes belonging to the period of François I. :—

1. The blind hermit Montanus visits the new-born Remi, who, touching him with his fingers wet with milk, restores his sight.

2. The hermit St. Remi, called by the people to the bishopric, receives the mitre.

3. Four miracles are performed by the saint: he extinguishes a fire lighted by demons in the city; he restores life to a girl; he is served at table by angels; when wine ran short at the table of his cousin Celsa, he blessed an empty cask, which was immediately filled.

4. The Battle of Tolbiac; Clovis instructed and baptized by Remi;

THE TENTH TAPESTRY OF ST. REMI, DAMAGED BY SHELL-SPLINTERS ON SEPT. 4, 1914

(*See description, pp.* 110, 111.)

the miraculous dove and an angel bring from heaven the Sacred Ampulla and the fleur-de-lys scutcheon.

5. Remi gives Clovis a cask of wine, telling him that he will always be victorious so long as the cask remains full ; a miller who refused to give his mill to the Church, sees his wheel turn the wrong way and his mill fall down ; St. Génebaud, Bishop of Soissons, punished by Remi for his sins, is afterwards delivered from his fetters by the saint.

6. The miracle of Hydrissen : Remi raises a man from the dead, who confirms his wish to leave a portion of his wealth to the Church, to the confusion of his son-in-law who contested the will.

7. Remi contemplating a heap of corn which he had collected to provide against famine, and which some drunkards had burnt. At a Council, Remi paralyses the tongue of a heretic priest, and then restores speech to him after repentance.

8. Remi, singing Matins in the chapel of the Virgin, is assisted by St. Peter and St. Paul and blessed by Mary. Remi, blind, dictates his will in the presence of St. Génebaud and St. Médard. Remi recovers his sight, celebrates mass and gives the Communion to his clergy. Remi dies and four angels carry away his soul.

9. Remi's funeral ; the procession goes towards the church of St. Timothy, where it is proposed to bury the saint, but in front of St. Christopher's, on the site of the present basilica, the saint, by making it impossible to lift his coffin, manifests his desire to be interred in this chapel. The saint's winding-sheet, carried in procession, dispels the plague that had been ravaging the city.

10. Angels transfer the relics of the saint to his mausoleum. A soldier who had tried to break in the door of the church, cannot withdraw his foot. Remi punishes the Bishop of Mayence, guilty of theft. Remi reveals himself with the Virgin and St. John. The Archbishop of Rheims, Robert de Lenoncourt, kneeling, presents the ten pieces of tapestry to the saint.

The latter tapestry was riddled with splinters (*photo, p.* 110) during the bombardment of September 4, 1914.

The Treasure

This was kept in the sacristy, the 15th century **carved wood** doors of which have Flamboyant style frames.

Formerly the richest of all the church treasures of France, it was impoverished in the course of the centuries, through wars and revolutions.

The **enamels** by Landin of Limoges (1633), dedicated to the lives of St. Timothy and St. Remi, a 12th century abbot's **crozier, reliquaries** and **sacerdotal ornaments** are noteworthy.

The treasure was removed, together with the doors of the sacristy, by the Historical Monuments Department.

The North Transept

Three small white marble Gallo-Roman or Carolingian capitals crown the colonnettes of the triforium.

Formerly, the church contained several tombs. Let into the wall of the north transept is a Latin epitaph, praising the virtues of a woman named Guiberge, who seems to have combined in her person the perfections of six women, *i.e.* the beauty of Rachel, the fidelity of Rebecca, the modesty of Susanna, the piety of Tabitha, the warm affections of Ruth, and the high morals of Anna.

THE RUINED TRANSEPT

In the foreground: Renaissance Balustrade round the Choir (*see p.* 115), *at the intersection of the Northern Transept. At the back: Inner side of the South Transept Door.*

The South Transept

The first chapel on the right of the apse, against the transept, is the chapel of St. Eloi.

In 1846, forty-eight storied flag-stones, taken from the flooring of the sanctuary of the church of St. Nicaise and collected by the architect Brunette, were placed there.

These 14th century lozenge-shaped stones are engraved in black, the hollowed-out portions being filled with lead. Each stone has a pretty border with a square medallion, in the middle of which two or three figures represent a scene from the Old Testament, from Noah to Daniel in the lions' den.

This chapel also contained two very expressive mediæval statues of painted wood and a 14th century Christ, all of which came from the old church of St. Balsamic.

The second chapel on the eastern side of the south transept contained an Entombment dating from 1531. In this group, which belonged to the old church of the Commandery of the Temple of Rheims, Joseph of Arimathea and Nicodemus hold the winding-sheet. Salome, and Mary the mother of St. James, stand near the tomb, while the Virgin, overcome with grief, is supported by St. John.

THE SIXTEENTH CENTURY ENTOMBMENT, FORMERLY IN ONE OF THE CHAPELS OF THE SOUTHERN TRANSEPT (*Cliché LL.*)

Facing this Burial Scene was the Altar-screen of the Three Baptisms, the work of Nicolas Jacques and the gift of Jean Lespagnol in 1610. This screen, which formed the background of the baptismal fonts, represented in three bas-reliefs : The baptism of Clovis (*on the right*), the baptism of Jesus by John the Baptist (*in the centre*), and the baptism of Constantine (*on the left*).

The railing round the baptismal fonts belongs to the second half of the 18th century, and was taken from the church of St. Pierre-le-Vieil.

SCULPTURED CONSOLES OF COLONNETTES IN THE CHOIR

The Choir of St. Remi Church

The Choir was rebuilt by Pierre de Celle. The plan is very like that of the choir of the Cathedral, of which it is the prototype.

As in the Cathedral, it intrudes upon the nave, of which it occupies the three last bays. In the latter, the columns placed against the six piers were removed. The groups of small columns which support the ribs of the vaulting rest upon a corbel-table carried by three consoles (*photo above*), which in turn rest on colonnettes with crocketed capitals. The central consoles are ornamented with figures of angels and symbolic animals, while under the lateral consoles are statuettes of prophets holding scrolls, on which their names are inscribed in painted letters.

Five circular radiating chapels open out on the vast ambulatory. The plan of the latter, like that of Notre-Dame-de-Châlons, evokes all that is most original in the Gothic architecture of Champagne. The bays with their alternations of square-ogival and triangular vaulting do not correspond with the breadth of the radiating chapels, which are connected to one another by three arcades resting on light columns. In the lower nave, from the curiously large number of points of support, it would seem that the builders had doubts as to the strength of the pointed style and, by way of precaution, greatly increased the number of points of support inside the church and of the exterior buttresses. The tribunes rising above the arcades are surmounted with a triforium lighted by high windows, which still retain their beautiful early 18th century stained-glass. The somewhat stiff figures stand out on a uniformly blue ground. In the upper part, apostles, evangelists, and the sixteen greater prophets are grouped around a stately Virgin. In the lower

FRAGMENT OF PASCHAL CHANDELIER DESTROYED BY THE BOMBARDMENTS OF 1914

part, the principal archbishops of Rheims on thrones are seated round St. Remi who occupies the place of honour below the Virgin. In the two last windows are effigies of Archbishops Samson (*deceased in* 1161) and Henry of France, during whose episcopate Pierre de Cello caused the apse to be built.

The choir is surrounded by a Renaissance railing which is out of harmony with the general scheme. It was erected between 1656 and 1669, at the joint expense of the widow of the famous barrister Omer Talon, the Town Council, the Duke of Longueville, and the Grand Prior of St. Remi. The sculptor François Jacques seems to have co-operated therewith.

The great *crown of light* hanging at the entrance to the choir was an imitation of the original crown, destroyed in 1793, and which was garnished with ninety-six candles, symbolizing the ninety-six years of St. Remi's life (*see p.* 108).

The 18th century high-altar of red marble which, like the cross and the six chandeliers, came from the church of the Minims, was crushed beneath the falling vaulting.

At the time of the Revolution (1792) the chandelier (masterpiece of the old Rheims metal-founders), which adorned the centre of the Sanctuary, was broken and melted down, with the exception of a portion of one of the feet. This fragment (*photo above*), preserved in the Archæological Museum, was destroyed by the bombardment of 1914.

TOMB AND RELIQUARY OF ST. REMI

The Tomb and Reliquary of St. Remi

The present tomb, erected in 1847, is only a memorial of the sumptuous mausoleum, profusely decorated with gold medals, diamonds and sapphires, which was destroyed at the time of the Revolution.

It is a Renaissance chapel, ornamented with the statues of the original tomb, which form by far the most interesting part of the monument. The twelve Peers are represented in their coronation robes: the Archbishop, Duke of Rheims, carries the Cross; the Archbishop, Duke of Laon, the sceptre; the Bishop, Count of Beauvais, the royal mantle; the Bishop, Count of Châlons, the ring; the Bishop, Count of Noyon, the girdle; the Duke of Burgundy, the crown; the Duke of Aquitaine, the standard; the Duke of Normandy, a second standard; the Count of Flanders, the sword; the Count of Toulouse, the spurs; the Count of Champagne, the military standard of the King.

The Reliquary of St. Remi, which is in the mausoleum, dates from 1896. It was bought by national subscription and presented to the church on the occasion of the centenary of the baptism of Clovis. In the niches of the lower part of the reliquary are statuettes of the twelve apostles. Higher up, in the recesses of the long sides, enamels illustrating episodes in the life of St. Remi are imbedded. On the two ends, two enamels represent the Battle of Tolbiac and the Baptism of Clovis.

Leave the Church of St. Remi by the western doorway, which faces the Place de l'Hôpital civil, cross the square, then turn to the right into the Rue Simon. The entrance to the Hôtel-Dieu Hospital *is on the right.*

The Hôtel-Dieu

This hospital is installed in the buildings of the ancient Abbey of the Benedictine monks of St. Remi who, for centuries, were the guardians of the relics of the famous Bishop of Rheims.

During the invasion, at the time of the Revolution, the Abbey was transformed into a military hospital, but it was only in 1827 that it became officially the *Hôtel-Dieu*, in place of the old Municipal Hospital (*see* "*Palais de Justice,*" *p.* 93). The furnishings of the latter were then transferred to the Abbey buildings, disaffected since the Restoration.

Of the ancient abbey, where *Charles-le-Simple* and the *Duc Robert* were proclaimed king, and where several archbishops were elected, only a few vestiges remain. Damaged by the fires of 1098, 1481, and 1751, it was completely destroyed by the great conflagration of January 15, 1774. The present abbey, rebuilt by Duroche, the King's architect, was scarcely finished when the Revolution broke out.

Incendiary bombs dropped by German aeroplanes in August, 1916, destroyed most of the buildings.

The monumental façade which faces the Court of Honour is Louis XVI. in style.

The second court, that behind the main buildings, is bordered by a cloister built by the Rheims architect, Nicolas Bonhomme, in the first part of the 18th century, in place of the 13th and 14th century cloister destroyed in 1707. The buttresses of the side which abuts on the church of St. Remi, and those of the opposite side, are 12th century.

The marble fountain with bronze furnishings, in the centre of the court, was formerly in the Place St. Nicaise. It was erected in 1750 from designs by *Coustou.*

THE CLOISTER AND FOUNTAIN OF THE HÔTEL-DIEU

THE GRAND STAIRCASE OF THE HÔTEL-DIEU
Through the windows is seen the North Front of St. Remi.

At the back of the court, on the left, is an exceedingly fine Louis XVI. staircase with wrought-iron handrail (*photo above*).

The **Lapidary Museum,** which was formerly in the crypt of the archi-episcopal chapel (*see p.* 65), was installed under one of the galleries of the cloister in 1896. Of the tombstones, storied floor-tiles, and various carvings which it contains, the most remarkable is the **Tomb of Jovinus.**

Consul in 367, Jovinus commanded the armies in Gaul, under the Emperor Julian, and successfully resisted three attempts at invasion by the Alemanni. As a Christian, he founded a basilica at Rheims.

The white marble tomb with carvings is apparently Græco-Roman of the 3rd century, and dates back before the time of Jovinus, who died in 370. It is possible that Jovinus had the first occupant of the tomb ejected, or that he bought an old sarcophagus and had his own portrait affixed to it.

The chapel installed in the old library of the abbey contained some fine Louis XVI. wood carvings (*see photo below of the ruins of the chapel*).

CHAPEL OF THE HÔTEL-DIEU IN 1919

THE OLD CHAPTER-HOUSE OF THE ABBEY

The **chapter-house** of the abbey, which served as a refectory, was rebuilt about the end of the 12th century. With its pointed arches, it belonged to the early period of Gothic architecture. The most remarkable portion was the vestibule facing the cloister. The deccration of the lateral arcades of the vestibule included Roman capitals, nearly all of which are intact (*photo below*), and which are of great value from the standpoint of the history of art and costumes. In the refectory were the *Godard* tables made out of a single branch of a gigantic oak-tree from the forest of St. Basle. They were given to the old *Hôtel-Dieu* by Canon Godard, whose name is incrusted in lead in the wood, as a rebus : *Go*, followed by the figure of a dart (French : *dard*).

Near the chapter-house, a round-arched chamber was all that remained of the early portion of the abbey.

ROMAN CAPITALS IN THE VESTIBULE OF THE CHAPTER-HOUSE

THE GRAND STAIRCASE OF THE HÔPITAL GÉNÉRAL

After visiting the Hôtel-Dieu, follow the Rue Simon, which skirts the Ecole de Médecine, then turn to the right into the Rue St. Remi. At the end of same, take the Rue Gambetta on the left, and follow it as far as the **Hôpital Général** *on the right.*

The Hôpital Général

This is the old Order-House of the Jesuits, built at the beginning of the 17th century. The **refectory** is ornamented with rich woodwork and paintings, by the Rheims artist Hélart. Of greater interest is the **library**, situated under the gables, and which is reached by a fine staircase. The room is adorned with a profusion of wood-carvings and mouldings. Exceedingly fine consoles carry the ceiling, whose carved panels are profusely ornamented with crowns, polygons, florets and heads of angels. The oaken pilasters which separate the bookshelves are decorated with a variety of leaves and flowers. In spite of this wealth of ornament, the general effect is harmonious. The recesses in the woodwork, opposite the dummy dormer-windows, were for reading.

Ancient vines cover the walls of the chapel, near the entrance to the *hôpital.*

At the side of the Hôpital Général stands the **Church of St. Maurice.**

This church was entirely rebuilt by the Jesuits after the destruction of the ancient edifice, which was one of the oldest in Rheims. Here may be seen the *Eagle Reading-Desk,* a fine piece of 17th century wood-carving; two *Louis XIV. portable iron desks* and the *paschal chandelier* of carved wood; the 17*th century confessionals* of the lateral chapels, and in the sacristy remarkable *Louis XIII., hand-embroidered guipures* of open-work designs, after the style of the models by the Rheims artist, Georges Baussonnet.

Return to the Place du Parvis, in front of the Cathedral, via the Rue Gambetta and its continuation, the Rue Chanzy.

A VISIT TO THE BATTLEFIELDS AROUND RHEIMS

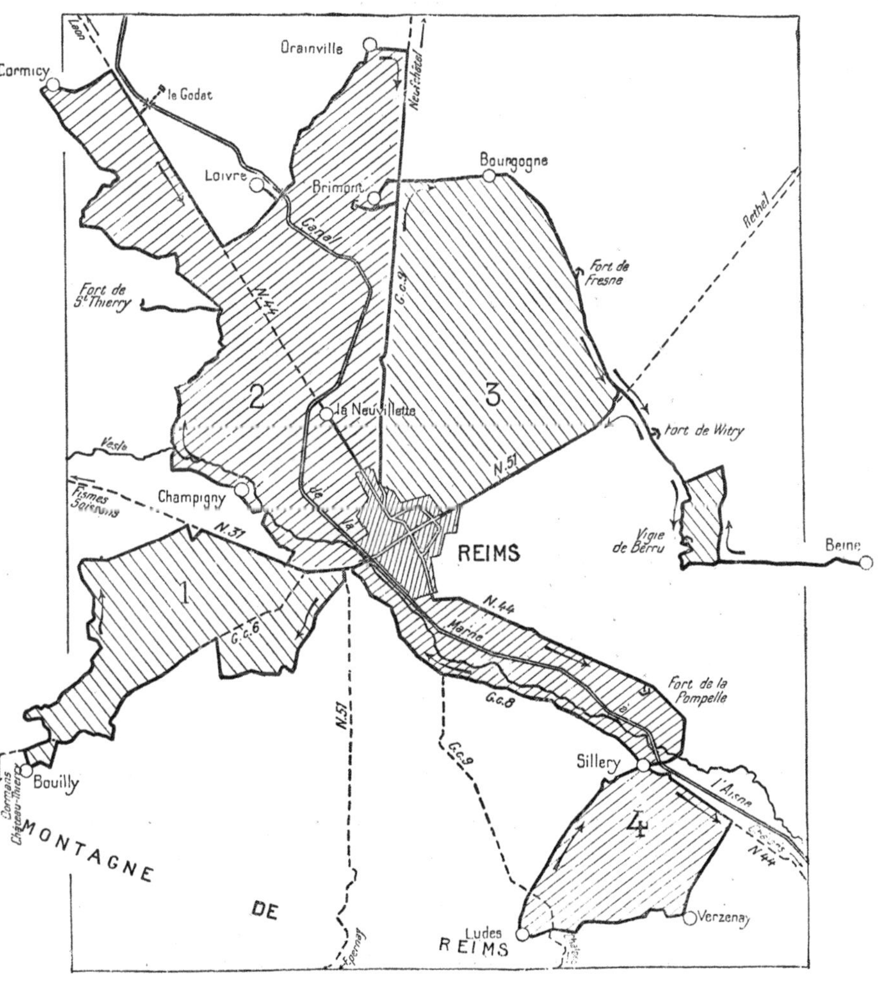

A thorough visit can be made in two days.

The Itinerary for each day is divided into two parts, to allow tourists to return to Rheims for lunch.

First Day	Morning	pp. 122–133.
	Afternoon	pp. 134–159.
Second Day	Morning	pp. 160-165.
	Afternoon.	pp. 166-174.

FIRST DAY

MORNING

THE MOUNTAIN OF RHEIMS

(See the complete Itineraries on p. 121, and the summary of the war operations on p. 131.)

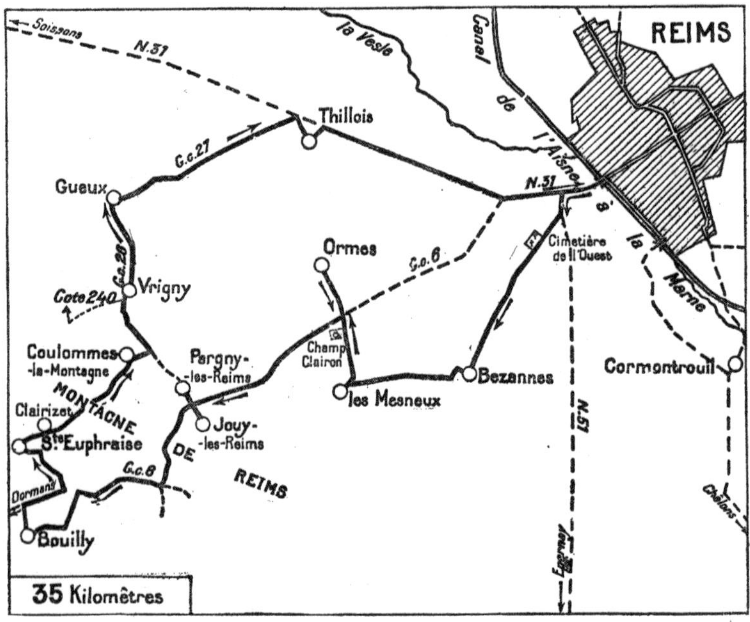

This part of the Itinerary will take the tourist to the most important points of the last German offensive of 1918, which aimed at the capture of Rheims.

Starting from the Place du Parvis Notre-Dame, take the Rue Libergier, opposite the Cathedral, turn to the right into the Rue Chanzy, follow same as far as the Rue de Vesle, take the latter on the left, and follow it to the end.

After the **Porte de Paris** *(see p. 68) the Rue de Vesle becomes the Avenue de Paris. Take same, but after passing under the railway bridge, turn to the left into the Avenue d'Epernay (R.N. 51, see plan, p. 121).*

Take the second street on the right (Rue de Bezannes), which passes in front of the **Western Cemetery,** devastated by the bombardments.

The road crosses numerous lines of trenches and boyaux, which defended the immediate approaches to Rheims.

Before reaching Bezannes village, leave on the right two roads which skirt a large estate enclosed with railings, go straight on to the ruined railway-station of Bezannes, then turn to the right.

Bezannes

(*See Itinerary, p.* 122.)

Cross the first group of half-ruined houses, then, on reaching a second group, which forms the main part of the village, turn to the left into the first street encountered, where the partially destroyed church *stands.*

The round-vaulted apse, tower, nave and aisles all belong to the Romanesque period. The Gothic doorway is 13th, and the spire of the belfry 15th century.

The square tower greatly resembles the old belfry on the doorway of St. Remi Church in Rheims, and, like the latter, dates apparently from the middle of the 11th century.

The Gothic doorway of the west front is set up against a Romanesque wall. The gable has been rebuilt in modern times. Vestiges of an ancient portal are to be found on each side of the doorway. The keystones of the arch above the tympanum, like those of the upper arching, are numbered in Roman figures, a peculiarity rarely to be found.

Facing the doorway of the church, on the left of the great entrance-door to a court, is a niche containing a 16th century stone **statue** representing a bishop wearing a chasuble.

In the court of the same house, over the door of the main structure, on the right, in an arched Renaissance niche, hollowed out and ornamented with marble incrustations, is the **statue** of a canon with folded hands kneeling at the foot of a crucifixion.

A shell-splinter took off the head of the bishop's statue, but the other group is intact.

Those interested in things prehistoric, may visit the **Pistat Collection** at Bezannes, which contains a great number of interesting specimens belonging to the stone and neolithic ages, and to the Gallic and Roman periods of the region.

Of the old castles of Bezannes, nothing of interest remains.

On September 11, 1914, during the Battle of the Marne, the German Staff took up their quarters in the house of M. Poullot. On the 12th, the battle attained the vicinity of the village.

Skirt the church, and at the cross-roads at the end of the village, keep straight on, past the cemetery on the right.

CHURCH OF BEZANNES IN 1914

The road climbs a small hill lined with trenches, then descends to the village of **Les Mesneux.**

At the entrance to this village (which is of no particular interest) turn to the right, and at the fork about fifty yards farther on, to the left, leaving the unmetalled road on the right.

About half-a-mile from Les Mesneux and shortly before reaching the crossing with the road to Rheims (*G.C.* 6), there is a small wood at the place called **Le Champ Clairon.** It was from here that German batteries under Colonel von Roeder fired on Rheims on September 4, 1914, in spite of the protestations of the Mayor of Les Mesneux, who assured the German commander that the French troops had completely evacuated the town.

At the crossing with G.C. 6, *keep straight on to Ormes,* whose church, at the entrance to the village, was almost entirely destroyed.

Ormes

(*See Itinerary, p.* 122.)

This village, in addition to numerous subterranean passages and chambers, possesses the interesting 12th century **Church St. Remi** (*photo below*).

Its circular apse with cornice resting on corbels is barrel-vaulted. Colonnettes in the great bays of the steeple (in ruins) carry carved 12th century capitals.

The pointed vaulting of the southern transept is 12th century, and the ogival groining rests on Norman capitals. The doorway of the western façade dates from the second half of the 12th century, and although its porch was destroyed in 1853 it is still remarkable.

THE CHURCH OF ORMES

THE INSIDE OF ORMES CHURCH

It comprises three tierce-pointed arcades surmounted by a line of billet-moulding. The lateral arcades are blind, while the higher central arcading around the door is surmounted with three receding *tori* resting on crocketed foliate capitals. The lateral arcades have similar capitals but only one *torus*.

Inside the church are interesting **16th century statues:** *St. Barbara* in stone and *St. Catharine*, painted and decorated, face the altar; *St. Remi* in stone, remarkable for its costume and decoration, stands above the altar of the northern chapel; a wooden *Virgin* surmounts the inner doorway.

ALTAR-SCREEN OF THE CHOIR

THE ROAD FROM RHEIMS TO JOUY, NEAR THE LATTER VILLAGE

Note the camouflaging.

Return by the same road to the crossing with the road to Rheims (*G.C.* 6), *where, opposite the* **Café du Joyeux Laboureur,** *turn to the right.*

The road rises towards the Mountain of Rheims. Of the *camouflaging* seen in above photograph, only traces remain.

Shortly after, the tourist passes between the villages of **Jouy** *and* **Pargny,** *whose houses border the road.* Jouy (*on the left*) and Pargny (*on the right*) were bombarded by the Germans in June, 1915.

The **Church of Jouy,** visible from the road to Rheims, was almost entirely destroyed.

To visit the church of Pargny, turn to the right opposite the grocery stores, No. 262, *then take the second street on the left* (near a fine mansion partly in ruins).

About 100 *yards farther on is* the church, the belfry of which was destroyed. *Return to the crossing with the main road to Rheims, where turn to the right.*

The road continues to climb the northern slopes of the Mountain of Rheims. On a hill to the left, the **Chapel of St. Lié** dominates the surrounding plain. There is a very fine view of Rheims from here.

The top of the rise is reached soon afterwards. Descend the southern slopes, passing between the sidings of an important material and ammunition depot situated on the reverse side of the mountain out of sight of the enemy's observation-posts. *On reaching the crossing half-way down the hill, leave on the left the two roads leading respectively to* **Ville Dommange** *and* **Courmas**

A short distance further on, after passing the road to Onrézy (*on the left*), *take the following narrow road on the left,* which passes between clumps of trees that were cut to pieces by shell-fire.

A little further on, on the right, is a cemetery containing the graves of some two hundred French, British and Italian soldiers.

Turn to the right after the cemetery. The road crosses a fine avenue bordered with shell-torn poplar trees, leading to the **Castle of Commetreuil** *on the left. The village of* **Bouilly** is reached soon afterwards.

THE END OF BOUILLY VILLAGE
(going towards St. Euphraise).

Bouilly—St. Euphraise—Clairizet

(*See pp.* 131–132, *and Itinerary, p.* 122.)

Bouilly was burnt by the Germans on September 12, 1914, under the pretext that the inhabitants had caused the death of two *Uhlans* killed the day before by French *Chasseurs.*

Turn to the right opposite the Church of Bouilly. There is a small cemetery on the right, just outside the village, containing several German graves.

On reaching G.C. 6, leading to Rheims, turn to the right. Take the first road on the left, which passes through a small devastated wood, where batteries of guns were posted. *Cross a small stream, and immediately afterwards the railway, then turn to the left into the village of* **St. Euphraise.**

Turn to the right in the village, opposite the church. The road rises steeply to the hamlet of **Clairizet**, which was almost entirely destroyed. *Pass by a* "Calvary," composed of four large trees surrounding a cross, *then turn to the left into a small narrow street.*

RUINED CHURCH OF ST. EUPHRAISE

COULOMMES VILLAGE SEEN FROM THE CHURCH

Coulommes-la-Montagne—Vrigny

(*See Itinerary, p.* 122.)

The road rises, then descends to **Coulommes-la-Montagne.** *Turn to the right at the entrance to the village.* The church, in ruins, is on the left.

At the cross-roads just outside the village take G.C. 26 *on the left. At first, the road dips rather abruptly, then rises to* **Vrigny.**

The Church of Vrigny, entirely in ruins, is on the right at the entrance to the village. *Pass the Town Hall, leaving a public washing-place on the left, then turn to the right.*

On leaving the village, take G.C. 26 *on the left to the village* of **Gueux.**

RUINS OF THE CHURCH AT VRIGNY

RUINS OF THE CHURCH OF GUEUX IN 1918

Gueux

(*See pp.* 131–132 *and Itinerary, p.* 122.)

Gueux is a small old-world village, with ancient houses, castle and church.

At the entrance to the village, a large square with trees, cut to pieces and devastated by the bombardment.

From the square, go to the **Church** *on the right,* now a heap of ruins. Seen through the trees from the square it forms a pitiful sight.

In the chapel, on the left of the main entrance, there was a fine piece of Renaissance carving.

It was to Gueux that the Archbishop of Rheims, Mgr. Luçon, betook himself after the bombardments of April, 1917. The village cemetery contains

GUEUX CHURCH IN 1917
Cardinal Luçon coming out of the Church (see above.)

THE ANCIENT CASTLE OF GUEUX

many soldiers' graves. The Cardinal-Archbishop of Rheims presided at a pathetic ceremony held during the War in honour of the dead.

To visit the **Castle**, *cross the square and take a small street on the left, which leads to the road to Rosnay* (*G.C.* 27).

Turn to the left, and fifty yards further on take on foot the narrow street on the left, which leads to the old castle.

This ancient castle, where the Kings of France, on their way to Rheims to be consecrated, used to dine, suffered severely from the bombardments. Outwardly it has, however, retained its general appearance (*photo above*).

Return to the car, and go straight on to the fork in the roads to Rosnay and Prémecy. Facing the fork is the entrance to the park and **modern Castle of Gueux,** belonging to the Roederer family, which was completely destroyed (*photo below*).

Turn the car round at the above-mentioned fork and continue straight along G.C. 27.

Beyond the village of Gueux the road crosses numerous lines of trenches. Many shelters and ammunition depots can still be seen along the road. *The National Road from Rheims to Soissons* (*N.* 31) *is reached soon afterwards. Near the cross-ways are the* ruins of an inn.

At this crossing, leave the National Road on the left and take the narrow road on the right which leads to **Thillois.**

THE MODERN CASTLE OF GUEUX

CROSSING OF THE THILLOIS AND RHEIMS ROADS

Thillois

(*See Itinerary, p.* 122.)

The **Church of Thillois** (late 12th century), now a heap of ruins, stood at the entrance to the village.

In 1914 it was still intact in all its vital parts. Its vaulting was pointed, with groining resting on columns, whose capitals were either Romanesque or Gothic. The nave had a timber roof.

The high-altar screen was a fine piece of sculptured stone-work of late 16th or early 17th century. In a niche above the altar, the Virgin, sitting on an X-shaped seat, was holding Jesus, clothed in a tunic and standing on her knee.

Leaving the church behind on the right, turn to the left, to reach the National Road. On the right is a small 18th century castle, behind a clump of fine stately trees, known as the *Bosquet de Thillois.* It was destroyed by shells.

Return to the National Road, turn to the right at the cross-roads, leaving on the left the road to Champigny, then return direct to Rheims, entering the city by the Avenue and Porte de Paris.

The Mountain of Rheims Battles

(*See p.* 14 *and p.* 122.

The fighting known as the *Battles of the Mountain of Rheims* took place in 1918 over the whole of the area described above, *i.e.* from Bouilly to Thillois, *via* St. Euphraise, Coulommes, Vrigny and Gueux (*see the Michelin Illustrated Guide : The Second Battle of the Marne*).

The Mountain of Rheims prolongs the region of Tardenois to the east. It is an important military position between the Vesle and the Marne, as it dominates the plain of Champagne. The higher part of it is finely wooded, while on the lower slopes and eastern and southern edges are the famous Champagne vineyards (*see Verzenay, pp.* 171–172).

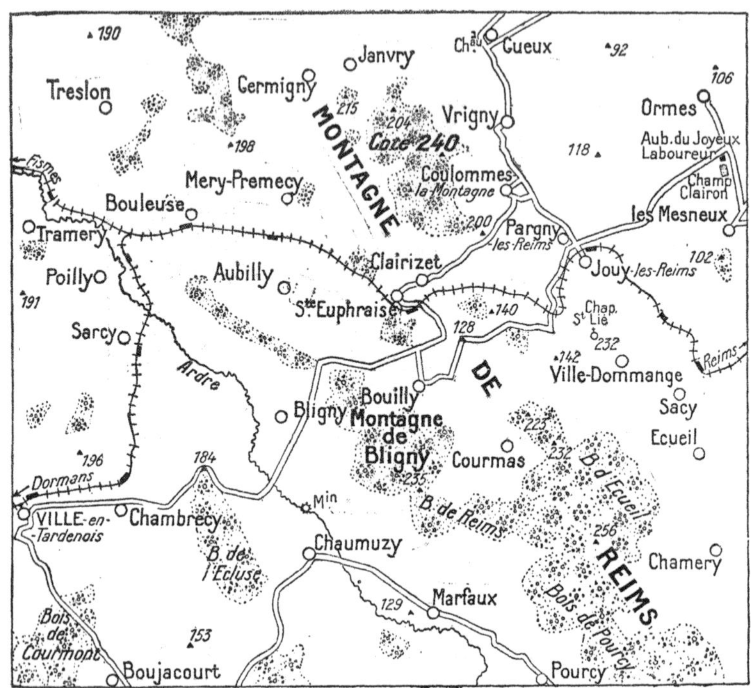

During the year 1918 the Germans made tremendous efforts to carry this position, the loss of which would have meant the fall of Rheims, leaving Epernay and Châlons-sur-Marne unprotected.

Although held to the east of Mountain, they obtained important successes on the west, where they reached the Marne, while in May they occupied the Woods of Courton and Le Roi. In July they crossed the Marne and advanced as far as Montvoisin, on the road to Epernay. Very fierce fighting took place, especially to the north-west of the Mountain at **Bouilly, Bligny, St. Euphraise** and **Vrigny.** These positions, and Hill 240 to the west of Vrigny, were several times lost and recaptured by the Allied troops under General Berthelot, French, Italian and British, who fought there side by side.

Vrigny was taken by the Germans on May 30, but retaken by the Allies on June 1 at the point of the bayonet. The same evening, four German regiments, after progressing slightly in the direction of Hill 240, were first checked, then driven back after bitter hand-to-hand fighting.

On June 9, the Germans were repulsed around Vrigny, after having sustained severe losses. On the 23rd, they rushed Bligny Hill, held by Italian troops, reaching the summit, but were shortly afterwards driven back. On the 29th, they sustained a like check at the same place.

In July they advanced their lines slightly towards Marfaux, Pourcy and Cuchery, but were unable to hold the captured ground. On the 18th, the Italians advanced in the region of Bouilly. On the 19th, Franco-British troops progressed towards St. Euphraise. On the 21st, the Allies carried Bouilly and St. Euphraise. On the 24th and 25th, in spite of desperate repeated efforts, the Germans were unable to hold Hill 240 which they had temporarily captured. On August 1 further enemy efforts to carry the Bligny uplands failed.

The region of Gueux—Thillois—Champigny was terribly ravaged by the war.

On September 11th, 1914, the French 5th Division, under General Mangin, drove the enemy from these positions, which remained in the French lines until May 30, 1918. Occupied by the Germans on May 31, after fierce fighting, they were completely devastated by artillery fire. Retaken by the French, then lost again in July, Thillois was finally recaptured on August 2, at the same time as Gueux.

On August 4, after having reached the Vesle at several points east of Fismes, French troops engaged a vigorous battle between Muizon and Champigny, and some of them succeeded in crossing the river the same day.

Champagne Wine

Wine-growing has always been a favourite industry in this part of France. The vineyards extend over the Rheims hills and along the valley of the Marne. In the hilly country around Rheims there are two distinct growths of wine: the *Montagne* proper, with its famous *Verzy*, *Verzenay*, *Mailly*, *Ludes*, *Rilly* and *Villers* "crus," and the *Petite Montagne* with its secondary "crus" of the *Tardenois Valley*, *Hermonville Hills*, *St. Thierry*, *Nogent l'Abbesse* and *Cernay-les-Reims*. The *Montagne* produces more especially black grapes for white wines.

Champagne wines were famous as far back as the 16th and 17th centuries. Henri IV. had a marked preference for the wines of *Ay*. The magnitude of the cellars still to be seen in the 16th and 17th century houses testifies to the importance of a trade, whose main outlets were Paris, Flanders, Belgium and Germany.

The Champagne wines of that period were red, and rivals of the famous Burgundy wines.

The vogue of Champagne wines as understood to-day dates back to the end of the 17th century. It was Dom Pérignon, cellarer of the Abbey of Hautevillers, near Epernay, who, if not actually the inventor of sparkling wines, first undertook to perfect them by blending the "crus" and preparing them with greater care.

In the last years of the reign of Louis XIV., and still more so under the Regency, the use of Champagne at Court gained ground, especially at the tables of the *Duc de Vendôme* and the *Marquis de Sillery*.

At that time Champagne was merely a "creamy" wine, *i.e.* semi-sparkling. The low breaking strain of the glass of those days would not have allowed of the higher pressure (six atmospheres) of the present-day wine. The discovery of the chemist François, who in 1836 at Châlons invented a special "densimeter," made it possible to calculate the amount of carbonic acid gas contained in the must, and to proportion the expansive force of the wine to the strength of the bottles, thus reducing losses by breakage, which for long had been very serious.

From the 19th century onwards, the production of Champagne wine has grown unceasingly. The number of bottles of sparkling Champagne placed on the market for sale in France and abroad rose from 19,145,481 (of which 16,705,719 went abroad) between April, 1875, and April, 1876, to 33,171,395 (of which 23,056,847 went abroad) between April, 1906 and April, 1907. During the first ten months of 1915, the exports of Champagne and sparkling wines were 630,140 wine-quarts, as against 1,092,660 wine quarts in 1914.

FIRST DAY

AFTERNOON

ST. THIERRY HEIGHTS—LE GODAT—THE GLASS-WORKS OF LOIVRE—BRIMONT—THE "CAVALIERS DE COURCY"

(*See complete Itineraries, p.* 121, *and summary of the military operations, pp.* 147 *and* 154.)

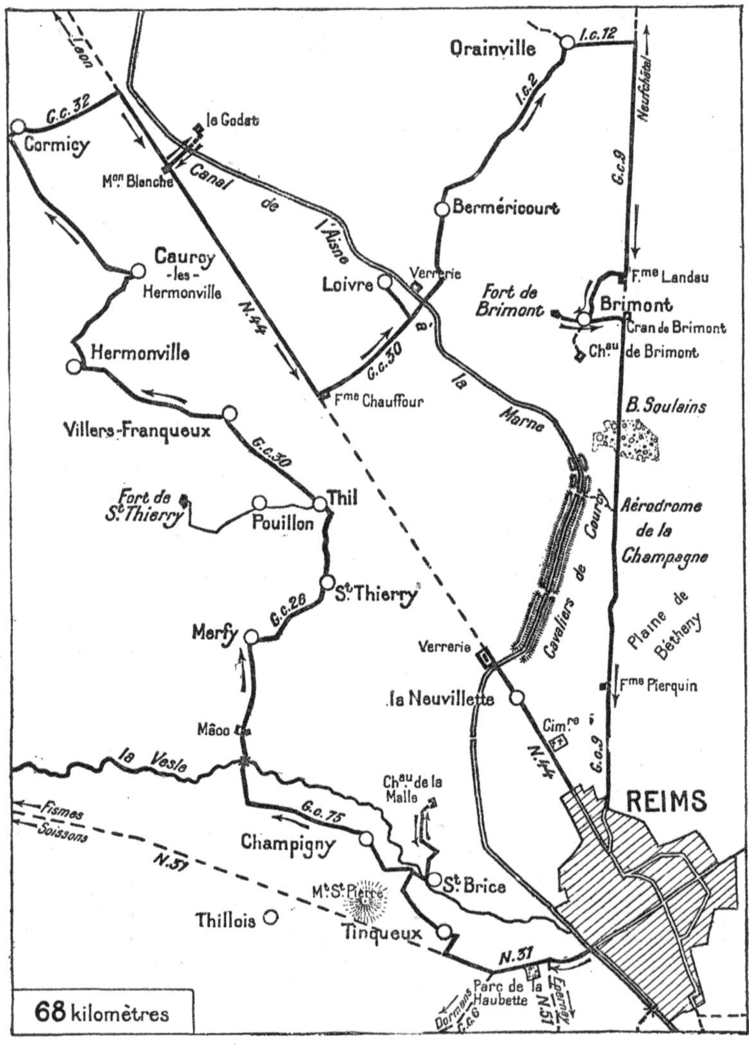

Starting from the Place du Parvis-Nôtre-Dame, follow the morning's Itinerary (*p.* 122) *as far as the railway bridge, then continue straight along the Avenue de Paris* (*N.* 31). *Before leaving Rheims the tourist can, if desired, visit* **Haubette Park.** *In this case, turn to the left, opposite No.* 10, *Avenue de Paris, into the Rue Flin des Oliviers. The entrance to* Haubette Park (an annex of the Calmette Dispensary) *stands at the beginning of this street, on the right.*

Napoleon I. bivouacked in this park while his troops attacked Rheims in 1814. A monument and a small museum commemorate the event. At the end of 1914 Haubette Park was a favourite recreation ground and refuge for the inhabitants of the city during the bombardments.

Return to the junction of N. 31 (*which leads to Fismes*) *with G.C.* 6 (*the road to Ville-en-Tardenois*). *Take N.* 31 *on the right. About* 1 *km. from the fork take the first road on the right.*

On reaching **Tinqueux** *turn to the left at the entrance to the village, and follow the main road.*

Tinqueux—Mont St. Pierre

The church of Tinqueux (St. Peter's) was entirely destroyed. It contained, on the left side of the nave, a remarkable 16th century painting on wood, representing the *Adoration of the Shepherds*, with a frame of the same period.

Near the church, between the Vesle and the main street of the village, stood an old baronial mansion, in front of which was a building with turreted façade known as the **Maison de la Salle.** Inside the buildings which, in later years, served as a farm, there was a curious old wooden staircase with railed balustrade. The whole was destroyed by the shells.

In September, 1914, at the beginning of the bombardment of Rheims, many of the people took refuge at Tinqueux.

At the end of the main street of the village, opposite a kind of observation-post with ladder in a tree, turn to the right. The road passes at the foot of **Mont St. Pierre,** whose village and church entirely disappeared in the 17th century.

THE MAIN STREET OF TINQUEUX VILLAGE

It was to replace the church of Mont St. Pierre that the church of St. Pierre de Tinqueux was built at the end of the 17th century.

The roads turns abruptly and nears the Vesle. Turn to the right and cross the river to reach **St. Brice.**

St. Brice--Champigny--Merfy

(*See Itinerary, p.* 134.)

Turn to the right at the entrance to the village and take the first street on the right, which leads to the church.

The Church of St. Brice was almost entirely destroyed. In style, it is

THE RUINED CHURCH OF CHAMPIGNY

Romanesque, with Renaissance doorway and aisles. The door of the west front contains interesting carvings—unhappily much mutilated.

Return by the same way to the cross-roads in front of the bridge over the Vesle, turn to the right, then, about 150 *yards further on, to the left. Continue straight ahead, cross the railway (l.c.) and follow the railway on the left.*

About half a mile further on an avenue on the right leads to the **Château de la Malle.** Both the castle and grounds were badly damaged by the bombardment.

Standing in the park with magnificent avenues of beech-trees, the castle is one of the most ancient manors in the vicinity of Rheims. It was rebuilt in one storey at the beginning of the 14th century on the old foundations. The decoration of the interior (Louis XVI.) is interesting. The drawing-room has retained its old wainscoting and paintings. A carved shield bearing the arms of the Cauchon family, a member of which, the Bishop of Beauvais, sided with the English and the Duke of Burgundy against the Dauphin of France and Joan of Arc during the Hundred Years' War, is still to be seen over a door of one of the out-buildings.

Return by the same road to the Vesle. Cross the river and follow it (as per Itinerary, p. 134), to the village of Champigny.

Cross straight through the village by the main street, at the end of which stands the church in a narrow by-street near the entrance to a park (photo, p. 136).

The little church of St. Theodule is 12th century, except the wooden belfry, which was modern. The belfry and roof were destroyed.

MERFY CASTLE, CONVERTED BY THE GERMANS INTO A BLOCKHOUSE

General Foch had his Headquarters there in 1914.

On leaving the village, go straight ahead. The road (G.C. 75) follows the railway on the left. Cross the railway (l.c.). The road passes along the marshy valley of the Vesle, then rises towards the St. Thierry Heights.

At the cross-roads of the hamlet of Mâco, *keep straight on along G.C. 26.* The road runs between two fairly high embankments containing numerous shelters. Slightly before entering the village of **Merfy** is a cemetery containing graves of French, British and German soldiers.

At the entrance to the same village, on the right, stands a castle, severely damaged, which, early in September, 1914, served as headquarters to General Foch (*photo above*).

A little farther is the church, almost entirely destroyed.

At the church, turn to the right and follow the main street, which is lined with houses in ruins.

On leaving Merfy, cross the railway (l.c.). The village of **St. Thierry** *is reached shortly afterwards.*

ENTRANCE TO ST. THIERRY VILLAGE
The sign and camouflaging are German.

ST. THIERRY CHÂTEAU IN 1914

ST. THIERRY CHÂTEAU IN 1919

ST. THIERRY CHURCH
See other photos, p. 140.

St. Thierry

(*See Itinerary, p.* 134, *and summary of the Military Operations, p.* 147.)

This village was frequently bombarded by the Germans from 1914 to 1918. *It is crossed by a narrow, winding street containing several sharp turnings. Shortly before the end of the village, the street widens abruptly. About a hundred yards further on is the church, while on the right a monumental door gives access* to the **Château of St. Thierry** (*photos, p.* 138).

This castle was built in 1777 by Mgr. de Talleyrand-Périgord, Archbishop of Rheims. It replaced the ancient abbey founded in the 6th century by St. Thierry, a disciple of St. Remi. Remains of the 12th century chapter-house, ogives, colonnettes and capitals, as well as an old chimney-piece, have been rebuilt into the kitchens. The spacious Louis XVI. drawing-room and the dining-room were likewise remarkable.

The church (*see photos above and on p.* 140) possessed certain remarkable features, *e.g.* the porch, nave and organ-loft. The 12th century porch had a 17th century pent-house roof.

Inside the church were Gothic stalls, and a 16th century bas-relief depicting *The Martyrdom of St.Quentin.*

The church is now in ruins.

Opposite the castle gate turn to the left into G.C. 26.

In the embankments along the road are numerous shelters, posts of commandment, ammunition depots, etc.

ST. THIERRY CHURCH (*see p.* 139)

RUINED PORTAL OF ST. THIERRY CHURCH

RUINS OF CHOIR, ST. THIERRY CHURCH

RUINS OF THIL CHURCH

Thil—Villers-Franqueux

(*See Itinerary*, *p.* 134.)

On reaching Thil, turn to the left at the entrance to the village. Go straight through.

The church, entirely in ruins, *stands at the end of the village, on a small eminence to the right.*

Half-way through the village, on the left, is a road which leads to the St. Thierry Fort, via the village of Pouillon.

The road from Thil to Cormicy was the starting-point of the communicating trenches which led to the first lines along the National Road No. 44 and along the canal from the Aisne to the Marne, during the long stabilisation period of the Berry-au-Bac—Rheims front. All along the road can still be seen, practically intact, the military works which were in the immediate rear of the front lines, viz., posts of commandment, depots, shelters, etc. At the present time, close to the destroyed villages, these shelters are being used by the people as habitations.

Beyond Thil, the road passes between two embankments. **Villers-Franqueux** *is soon reached.* The ruined village and church *are somewhat to the right.*

RUINS OF VILLERS-FRANQUEUX

RUINED
CHURCH OF
HERMONVILLE

Hermonville

Follow the rails, straight ahead, to Hermonville.

Turn to the left, at the entrance to the village, into the large square, on the opposite side of which stands the **Town Hall**, partially destroyed. *The* **Church** *is on the right.*

This remarkable church is 12th century. The pointed vaulting of the nave was raised in 1870, but this had been provided for in the original plans. At the intersection of the transept the pointed vaulting is lower. The capitals with their finely carved palm-leaves appear to be rather more recent than those of the nave, and extend frieze-like round the pillars. The bays of the transept-arms and of the two square eastern chapels are round-arched and surmounted with a quatrefoil—an arrangement frequently met with in the vicinity of Rheims.

The outer porch, like that of Caurcy-les-Hermonville and St. Thierry, is a 12th century addition. The depressed arch of the entrance is 17th century.

The square tower at the corner of the nave and south transept has cubic capitals in the twin bays of the second storey.

The ancient **cemetery**, which used to surround the church, is bordered by old houses. Entrance was gained by a little gate facing the porch, in which are incrusted fragments of a 15th century altar-screen representing a horseman and a group of persons.

The village was frequently bombarded by the Germans after the Battle of the Marne. In 1916 several inhabitants were killed by shells.

Leave the church on the right, and follow the Rue Sébastopol, at the end of which is an abrupt turning to the left. The road skirts a large house and garden surrounded by a wall. At the end of the latter, turn to the right into the Rue de Sommerville. On leaving the village, turn to the left, then go straight on to **Cauroy-les-Hermonville.**

CAUROY CHURCH IN 1914

Cauroy-les-Hermonville

Turn to the right at the entrance to the village, then into the first street on the left, where stands the half-destroyed **Church of Nôtre-Dame.**

This Church (*historical monument*) has an original 12th century porch, which was mutilated by the bombardments.

Romanesque in style, it stands out from the remainder of the building and extends over the whole breadth of the west front. Its tile-covered roof rests on a timber-work frame, whose beams appear to be 16th century. Two round-arched openings in the ends of the porch serve as entrances. The front is pierced with a number of round arcades. The central door giving access to the church is of a later date (16th or 17th century). The capitals of the arcadings are 12th century. Their curious decoration represents figures of men, animals, birds scrolls, etc.

The ruined tower and nave were likewise 12th century. The side-chapels, transept-crossing and choir were rebuilt in the 16th century.

CAUROY CHURCH IN 1918

STREET IN CAUROY VILLAGE

(Seen from the Porch of the Church. To go from Cauroy to Cormicy, take this street opposite the Church.)

In the interior of the church, the wooden altar-screen over the high-altar dated from 1616. The painting which decorated its central panel, and the side wood-work of the choir were removed in 1888. The altar-screen (1547) of the southern side-chapel was composed of an assemblage of stone statues representing *The Virgin carrying Jesus*, *St. Roch, a pilgrim*, and *St. Stephen, a deacon, with the donor kneeling at his feet.*

Under several of the houses in the village are subterranean passages, the most noteworthy being that under the old presbytery on the left of the church, to which access is gained by a stair of fifty-one steps.

Leave the village of Cauroy by the street (*photo, p.* 145) *which opens up opposite the church.*

The road passes through clumps of devastated trees. *On the left side of the road is* a cemetery, containing numerous well-organised shelters. *The village of* **Cormicy** *is next reached.*

Cormicy

(*See Itinerary, p.* 134.)

Turn to the right at the entrance to the village. On either side are tree-lined boulevards, which were made on the ancient ramparts. The trees have been cut to pieces by the shells.

Cormicy was formerly a small fortified town with turret, gates, ramparts and moats, all of which have disappeared except one gate. The site was planted with trees, which surround practically the whole town. The town was destroyed in the time of Charles VI., during the Hundred Years' War.

The present village suffered severely during the German bombardments, most of the houses being damaged. In June, 1916, only eighty-three inhabitants remained in their homes.

CORMICY CHURCH IN 1914

The ancient **Church** was likewise badly damaged (*photos above and below*). While the tower, west front, and the two first bays of the nave are late 15th or early 16th century, the greater part of the nave is 11th or 12th century. The chevet and the transept-crossing are early 13th century, while the transept ends probably date from the middle of 12th century.

The portal comprises twin doors surmounted with a broad flamboyant recess. The doors have been partially mutilated. Above the window

CORMICY CHURCH IN 1918

G.C. 32 ROAD ON LEAVING CORMICY
(*See Itinerary*, p. 134.)

runs a balcony, the Gothic balustrade of which, known as the *Gloria Gallery*, was modern. This balustrade was destroyed by the bombardments, which also brought down the steeple.

The west front has two Gothic doors with 16th century iron-work, at the extremity of the aisles. The tympana of these doors, formerly lighted, have been bricked up. The lintels have three consoles ornamented with fantastic animals and banderoles. The three statues which carried the consoles have long since disappeared.

In the south transept, on the left, behind the altar, is an interesting small door surmounted with a square lintel of the 11th or 12th century. Two figures of winged monsters with heads of a man and a woman and fish tails, stand out in high relief, framed and separated by a belt, on which are carved *florets* mingled with fantastic figures.

The three remarkable 18th century marble altars of the choir and transept chapels come from the Church of the Nuns of Longueau, the abbey of which, in the Rue du Jard at Rheims, was sold in 1790. The high-altar occupies nearly the whole of the chancel. Over the tomb, six columns of grey Dinant marble, crowned with Corinthian capitals, support an oval marble cornice with richly carved and gilt consoles of wood. The very large, white and gilt tabernacle is a fine example of 17th or 18th century wood-work. Its door, decorated with symbolic attributes, is surrounded by statuettes depicting, *in the lower part*, St. John the Evangelist and a holy woman wearing crowns; *above each of these figures*, an angel; *at the top*, The Resurrection of Christ.

The sixteen carved oak stalls of the choir, as well as the wrought-iron reading-desk on a marble pedestal, also came from the former Abbey of Longueau.

Near the choir, on a pillar of the nave, is an inscription to the effect that the chronicler *Flodoard*, who died in 966, was *Curé* of Cormicy.

The modern **Town Hall**, built by the Rheims architect, Gosset the elder, which faced the church, was entirely destroyed.

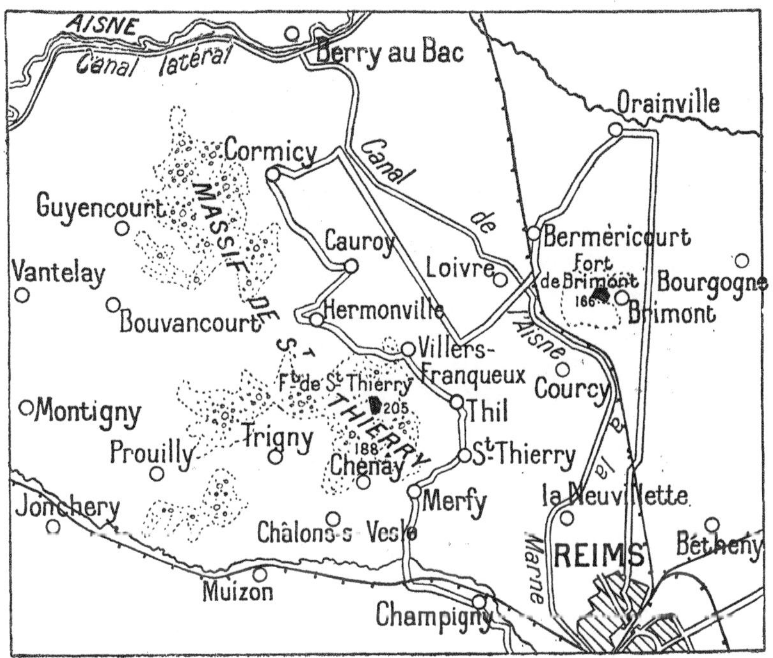

All the places visited since leaving Merfy, *i.e.* St. Thierry, Thil, Villers-Farnqueux, Hermonville and Cormicy, border the St. Thierry Heights. The latter are commanded by the fort of the same name and the Chenay Redoubt, with altitudes of about 670 and 620 feet respectively. They were recaptured from the Germans after the Battle of the Marne on September 11, 1914, by the French 3rd Corps.

After the loss of the Chemin-des-Dames and the Aisne Canal on May 27, 1918, this position, which with its guns commands the road and railway from Rheims to Soissons and the road from Rheims to Laon, remained the sole protection of Rheims to the north-west.

It was defended by the French 45th Infantry Division (General Naulin), composed of Algerian Sharp-shooters, Zouaves and African Light Infantry, who held their ground on May 27–28, after which they were reinforced by battalions of Singalese and Marines drawn from the sector east of Rheims.

The struggle was a fierce one, and hand-to-hand fighting frequent. Finally the constant inflow of German reserves forced back the French, who, on May 29, had to abandon the position, to which the enemy afterwards clung for four months. On October 1 the Germans, beaten on the previous evening by the French 5th Army on the high ground between the Aisne and Rheims, was forced to retreat. The French regained possession of Merfy and St. Thierry, and advanced as far as the outskirts of the Fort of St. Thierry, which, with Thil and Villers-Franqueux, Hermonville, Courcy and Cormicy, fell into their hands in the course of the next few days (*see map above*).

DESTROYED BRIDGE OVER THE CANAL, NEAR LE GODAT

From Cormicy to Godat Farm

(*See Itinerary, p.* 134.)

Pass straight through Cormicy, leaving the church on the left. Take G.C. 32 *to the Rheims-Laon road (N.* 44), *where turn to the right. Rather less than a mile further on, near the* Maison Blanche, *is a road leading to* **Godat Farm.** *Cars can only go as far as the canal,* the destroyed bridge (*photo above*) not having yet been rebuilt. The lock-keeper's house *seen in the photograph below* was completely destroyed.

Cross the canal on foot to reach Godat Farm, situated about 300 *yards further on.*

Le Godat, formerly a small fief with a castle and chapel (destroyed during the Revolution in 1793), was merely a farm and a plain country house when

THE LOCK-KEEPER'S HOUSE AT LE GODAT

(*Now destroyed.*)

RUINS OF LE GODAT FARM

the war broke out. By reason of its position, north of the Aisne Canal, this bridgehead was, throughout the war, one of the most fiercely disputed points in the sector north-west of Rheims, even during the period of trench-warfare. At the time of the French offensive of April, 1917, the 44th Infantry Regiment advanced beyond Le Godat, where the French held their ground until the powerful German push of May 27, 1918.

The farm is now a mere heap of ruins. Shelters still exist in the basements.

Return to the National Road, and turn to the left.

The road crosses numerous boyaux which provided access to the front-line trenches down the hill on the right.

Follow the National Road to **Chauffour Farm** (in ruins), *where take the road on the left to* **Loivre.**

On nearing the canal, the ruins of the village of Loivre (entirely destroyed) *become visible.*

EMPLACEMENT OF GERMAN HEAVY GUN AT LOIVRE

RUINS OF THE CHURCH AT LOIVRE

From Loivre to Brimont

Loivre.—*Visit the village on foot. The canal can only be crossed near the lock south-east of the village.* The destroyed bridge has been replaced by a temporary footway across the bed of the canal, which necessitates climbing down and up the banks by steep paths.

After crossing the canal the tourist passes by the ruins of the Loivre Glass-Works, founded in 1864 by the descendants of the noble house of Bigault de Grandrupt, glass manufacturers of Argonne.

Loivre and its glass-works were occupied in September, 1914, by the Germans, who deported the inhabitants to the Ardennes. The village and works

GENERAL VIEW OF THE RUINS AT LOIVRE IN 1919

SEPULCHRE IN THE CEMETERY AT LOIVRE, USED BY THE GERMANS AS A PHOTOGRAPHIC DARK-ROOM

were re-captured during the offensive of April 16, 1917, by the French 23rd and 133rd Infantry Regiments, surnamed *Les Braves* and *Les Lions* respectively. Whilst other battalions outflanked the village and crossed the canal, the third battalion of *Lions* attacked it in front. The position, powerfully organised, was stoutly defended. The attacking troops were obliged to come to a halt in front of the cemetery (a veritable bastion with concrete casemates), and before the ruins of the mill, both of which bristled with machine-guns. Withdrawing slightly to allow of a barrage of 75's, they rushed forward again under the protection of the latter. The site of the mill and the cemetery were captured, together with numerous prisoners (122 were taken in one machine-gun shelter). The ruined village was next carried in a bayonet charge, to the sound of the bugles. The captures were considerable, one battalion of 500 men alone taking 825 prisoners.

In March and May, 1918, two violent attacks were made on Loivre by the Germans, but without success. They took it on May 27, only to be driven out on October 4.

Before the war, a road, which has since completely disappeared, *led direct from Loivre to Brimont. To reach the latter it is now necessary to go farther north, via Berméricourt and Orainville, returning southwards by the Neufchâtel to Rheims road (see Itinerary, p.* 134).

Berméricourt.—This hamlet, of Gallo-Frankish origin, was formerly more populous. The bombardments have literally wiped it out.

From Berméricourt the tourist reaches **Orainville** *by G.C.* 30, *which becomes I.C.* 2 *after crossing the boundary line between the " departments " of the Marne and the Ardennes. At the entrance to the ruined village, near the church, turn to the right into I.C.* 12, *which,* 1 *kilometre further on, joins the road from Neufchâtel to Rheims (G.C.* 9), *where turn to the right.*

Follow this road for four and a half kilometres to the ruins of **Landau Farm,** *turn to the right, then, about* 200 *yards further on, take the road on the left to the* village of Brimont, entirely destroyed.

ALL THAT REMAINS OF BERMÉRICOURT VILLAGE

Brimont Fort and Château

(*See Itinerary, p.* 134, *and summary of the Military Operations, p.* 154.)

Situated to the west of the road from Rheims to Neufchâtel (formerly a Roman causeway which crossed the hill at *Cran de Brimont*) Brimont was already important in Roman times. It was fortified in the Middle Ages, and traces of its ancient fortifications are still to be found on the hill. The discovery of a Roman tomb in 1790 caused considerable excitement in archæological circles, as it was believed to be the burial-place of the Frankish Chief *Pharamond* who, according to one chronicler, had been buried on a hillock near Rheims.

In 1339, during the siege of Rheims by the English, the Duke of Lancaster had his camp at Brimont.

RUINS OF BRIMONT VILLAGE

In the foreground, on the left: Road to Brimont Fort. On the right: Beginning of the road to the Château (entirely destroyed).

RUINS OF THE CHURCH OF BRIMONT

On several occasions, since September, 1914, the Germans deported the inhabitants of Brimont and Coucy to the Ardennes. The village is now destroyed and its church a heap of ruins.

The church was built at the beginning of the 15th century.

The four last bays of the nave, which was partly Romanesque, were altered in the middle of the 16th century.

The sacristy occupied the lower storey of the square, pointed-arch tower.

Several ancient statues were placed at the entrance to the Choir: *St Remi*, with a woman in late 15th century dress kneeling at his feet; a *Virgin* offering grapes to the Infant Jesus in her arms (late 15th century) and a large *Christ Crucified*, dated from the middle of the 16th century. A beautiful 18th century *lectern* of carved wood, representing an eagle standing on a massive three-sided pedestal of red and white marble, stood in front of the Choir.

BRIMONT FORT

To visit the **Fort of Brimont,** *skirt the church on the side of the portal staircase, then take the road seen on the photograph on p.* 152. *The Fort is about* 400 *yards further on.*

The Defences North of Rheims and the Fighting in that Sector

The **Fort of Brimont,** completed by the **Battery of the Cran de Brimont** about a mile to the east, and on the west by the **Loivre Battery,** mentioned on page 151, sweeps the whole country north of Rheims as far as

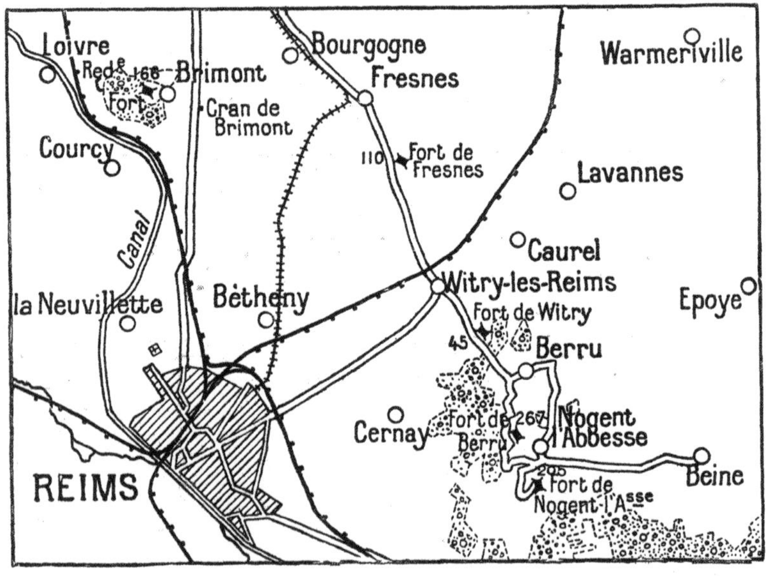

The roads shown on the above map are those followed by the Third Itinerary (see p. 160).

the banks of the Aisne, Suippe, Retourne and the Aisne-Marne canal, the Rheims-Neufchâtel, Rheims-Vouziers, Rheims-Rethel and Rheims-Laon roads, and the Rheims-Laon and Rheims-Charleville railways. About five miles east of Brimont and four miles east of Rheims is the position of **Berru** (*see p.* 165), extending along a front of about six miles, *via* the hills of Berru and Nogent l'Abbesse. Intended by those who planned it to guard the valley of the Suippe, the Rheims-Rethe and Rheims-Vouziers roads, as well as the Rheims-Charleville and Rheims-Châlons-sur-Marne railways, it comprises the **Fort of Witry** (about 150 feet in altitude), the batteries of **La Vigie de Berru** (870 feet), and the **fort and batteries of Nogent-l'Abbesse** (670 feet).

Brimont and Berru are further covered and linked up by the **Fort of Fresne** (360 feet), situated four miles north-east of Rheims.

These defensive works, conceived and executed after the war of 1870, had, in consequence of the evolution of strategical and tactical doctrines, been abandoned or disarmed before the war of 1914. After evacuating Rheims on September 12, 1914, the Germans grasped the importance of these works, to which they clung tenaciously, after hurriedly organising them. It was against these naturally strong positions, further strengthened by trenches, that the French 5th Army, in pursuit of the enemy, found themselves brought to a standstill on the evening of September 12. From September 13 to 18, the French tried in vain to capture them. The 5th Division, under General Mangin, did succeed in capturing the **Château de Brimont,** in the plain, but were unable to hold it.

Later, the Germans converted these hills into one of the most formidable positions organised by them in France. Brimont, Berru, Fresne and Nogent l'Abbesse, whose guns slowly destroyed Rheims, were, so to speak, her jailers for four years.

In April, 1917, during the French offensive of the Aisne, one division, known as the "Division of aces" (because its four regiments have the fourragère decoration), penetrated into Berméricourt and advanced to the outskirts of Brimont, but was unable to hold its ground against the furious counter-attacks of the Germans. It was only in October, 1918, that the French 5th Army, in conjunction with the victorious attacks of the 4th Army in Champagne, after forcing the Germans back to the Aisne and the canal, and after crossing the Aisne canal on October 4 in front of Loivre and near Berméricourt, forced the enemy, whose communications were now threatened, to abandon one of the most valuable portions of his 1914 positions. On October 5, the French re-entered Brimont and Nogent l'Abbesse, progressed beyond Bourgogne, Cernay-les-Rheims, Beine, Caurel and Pomacle, and, in spite of desperate enemy resistance, drove back the Germans to the Suippe.

After visiting the fort return to the village of Brimont.

From here the **Château de Brimont** may be visited, but this will have to be done on foot as the road has been destroyed, traces only of it being left in places (*the lower photograph on p. 152 shows the beginning of the road in the village*).

The **Château de l'Ermitage,** also known as the Château de Brimont, *is situated about* 500 *yards south of the village, at the entrance to a* large park, completely devastated. It was the scene of desperate fighting (*see p.* 152).

Return to Brimont, cross the village (skirting the church and continue straight on to the **Cran de Brimont Redoubt** *on the road to Rheims.* Numerous German trenches, etc., are to be seen here.

Turn to the right into G.C. 9, *which dips down to the* Plain of Rheims. The region hereabouts bristle with barbed-wire entanglements and is crossed with numerous trenches. It was ranged to an incredible degree by the bombardments.

At the bottom of the hill which starts at the Cran de Brimont, cross Soulains Wood, of which only a few torn tree-stumps remain.

Several hundred yards after leaving the wood, take on foot the broken road to the **"Cavaliers de Courcy,"** situated *on the right, about* 500 *yards further on.*

THE AISNE CANAL AT THE "CAVALIERS DE COURCY"

The "Cavaliers de Courcy"

To the north of La Neuvillette, the Aisne-Marne Canal is flanked on both sides by enormous artificial embankments planted with fir-trees and known as the **"Cavaliers de Courcy."** After their retreat in September, 1914, the Germans entrenched thenselves there and clung to the east bank until April, 1917.

On April 16, 1917, the French 410th Regiment of the Line attacked the enemy's formidable positions there. This Brittany regiment set out from positions to which they had given names taken from the history of their country (*Quimper Bastion*, *Auray*, *Redon Bastion*, etc.). On the first day they carried three successive lines of defences, and advanced about a mile. On the 17th and 18th they left their zone of action, to ensure the *liaison* on their right, and to help a brigade in difficulties on their left. For eight days they held their positions against powerful enemy counter-attacks, after having progressed to a depth of two miles and captured more than 400 prisoners, 11 bomb-throwers, and an immense amount of stores.

These positions, like the neighbouring villages, were re-taken by the Germas in May and June, 1918, and finally by the Allies in October, 1918.

Return to the road and follow it towards Rheims. Leave on the left the devastated **Aviation-ground of Champagne**—now in a state of complete upheaval, due to the terrific shelling it received—*then cross the* **Plain of Bétheny** (*photo, p.* 157).

The Plain of Bétheny was the scene of two important historical events: in 1901 the Tsar Nicolas II, reviewed a part of the French Army there; in August, 1909, the Great Aviation Week was inaugurated there, in the presence of an immense crowd of spectators.

GERMAN FIRST-LINE POSITIONS IN BÉTHANY PLAIN (*see sketch-map below*)

Photographed at 7,000 ft. from aeroplane, August 6, 1916, at 10 a.m.

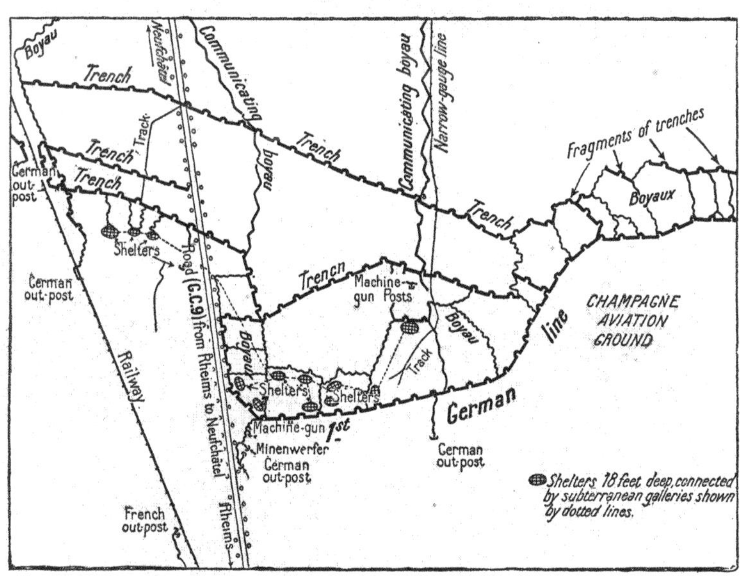

THE GERMAN FIRST-LINE DEFENCES IN THE PLAIN OF BÉTHENY

The tourist passes through this region on returning to Rheims, shortly before coming to the bridge under the railway. The sketch map explains the photograph above.

Pass under the Rheims-Laon railway by a very sharp double turning. **Pierquin Farm**, entirely destroyed, *stood on the right a short distance further on.* The only remaining trace is the torn shapeless carcass of a large iron shed.

The railway embankment south of Pierquin Farm was fiercely disputed from September 18, 1914, onwards. Several enemy attacks against it broke down before the French 75's. During the offensive of May, 1918, the whole of this region was the scene of desperate fighting. La Neuvillette was taken on May 30, and Pierquin Farm on the 31st. On August 4, the French, after crossing the Aisne Canal, advanced to La Neuvillette, where the enemy made a desperate stand. At the beginning of October they advanced to the north of La Neuvillette, which the enemy was eventually compelled to abandon. The last inhabitants had left the locality on July 12, 1916.

The tourist enters Rheims by the Rue de Neufchâtel and the Avenue de Laon.

La Neuvillette

On reaching the Avenue de Laon, the tourist, instead of entering Rheims, may turn to the right and go northwards as far as the village and cemetery of La Neuvillette.

The cemetery of La Neuvillette *is on the right of the road, between the last houses of Rheims and the village.* It was completely cut up by a network of first-line trenches (*photos, p.* 159).

The village of La Neuvillette, now in ruins, was the scene of desperate fighting during the German offensive of May, 1918.

Nothing remains of the 12th century church of John-the-Baptist.

The glass-works north-west of the village, by the side of the canal, are now a heap of ruins (*photo, p.* 159).

Return to Rheims by the same road.

THE ROAD TO RHEIMS AT NEUVILLETTE

THE GLASS-WORKS AT NEUVILLETTE

DRESSING-STATION AT NEUVILLETTE

THE CEMETERY AT NEUVILLETTE

SECOND DAY

MORNING

FRESNES FORT—WITRY-LES-REIMS—BERRU—NOGENT L'ABBESSE—BEINE

(*See complete Itineraries, p.* 121, *and map on p.* 154.)

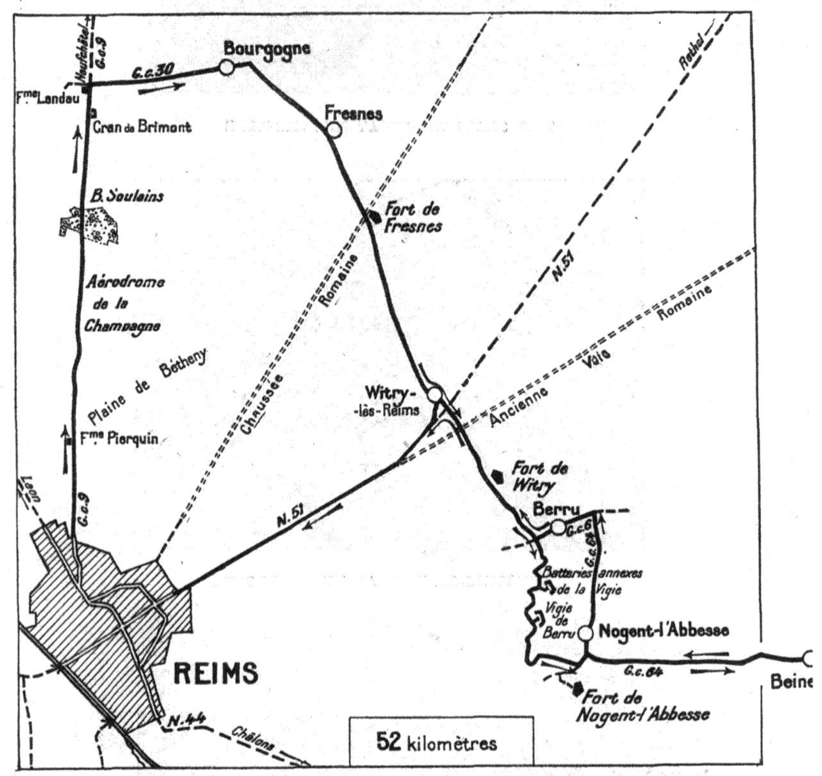

This Itinerary will lead the tourist through the region of the Forts to the north-east of Rheims, which formed the rear of the German lines during the stabilisation period of 1914–1918.

It was this line of forts that, in the German hands, held the French in check after the first Battle of the Marne. Practically the whole of these works were but little damaged by the relatively light bombardments, and have retained traces of the German organisation.

Leave Rheims by the Avenue de Laon (which begins at Les Pomenades, *opposite Mars Gate), and the Rue de Neufchâtel (second street on the right), Sortie No. IX. of the Michelin Tourist Guide (see coloured plan, pp.* 32–33).

RUINS OF THE CHURCH AT BOURGOGNE

Follow in the contrary direction the route described in the preceding Itinerary (p. 134 *to p.* 159) *as far as the crossing in the Berméricourt-Bourgogne road, where stood* Landau Farm, now entirely in ruins. *At this crossing take G.C.* 30 *on the right.* German camouflaging is still visible on the right-hand side of the road.

Bourgogne—Fresnes

The village of Bourgogne, entirely in ruins, *is soon reached.*

The village is of very ancient origin. Formerly it was protected by a belt of moats, now partly filled in, and by earthern ramparts, almost everywhere levelled. The lines of these moats, planted with rows of elm-trees, are clearly distinguishable. There is a very extensive view from this original site.

A portion of the village was burnt by the Germans who, in 1916, destroyed the belfry of the church with dynamite.

This church (dedicated to St. Peter and St. Paul), with its fine Romanesque tower, was remarkable.

The greater part of it dated from the 12th and 13th centuries. It is now in ruins (*photo above*).

Cross straight through the village. Numerous German signs *are still to be seen. At the cross-roads just outside the village, follow the railway, then cross it near the destroyed railway station of Fresnes. The village of* Fresnes *is reached shortly afterwards.*

Turn to the right at the first crossing met with. The church *stands about* 100 *yards away, on the left.*

Norman in style, the Church of Fresnes comprises a central nave with aisles and a tower without transept. It dates back to the 12th century, but was several times extensively altered and restored both in the 18th century and in recent times.

A small porch of limestone added to the northern aisle, is reached by a

RUINED CHURCH OF WITRY-LES-REIMS

round Norman bay of stone. In the corner of the porch, to the left on entering, is incrusted a fragment of a small funerary monument of the 16th century.

This church was almost entirely destroyed.

After turning to the right at the crossing mentioned above, keep straight on.

About 2 kilometres from Fresnes the road from that village to Witry-les-Reims crosses an old Roman causeway, at the side of which, slightly to the south of Hill 118, the Fort of Fresnes was built in 1878. This fort was blown up by the Germans during their retreat in 1918. Its ruins are impressive. In the moats of the fort are German trenches and shelters extending right up to the walls of the fort.

The village of Witry-les-Reims is next reached. It suffered severely from the numerous bombardments, which its situation near the first lines rendered inevitable.

Witry-les-Reims

After crossing the railway (l.c.) at the entrance to the village, keep straight on. The ruined church *is on the left, near the entrance to the village.*

Except for one tower, which dates from the 12th century, the church is modern. The spire was destroyed by the Germans. The belfry, used by the enemy as an observation-post, was struck by French shells.

Like many of the villages around Rheims, Witry-les-Reims is of Gallo-Roman origin. More than two hundred Gallic sepulchres and cinerary urns have been brought to light. The objects thus discovered, including a large number of vases, now form the *Bourin* pre-historic collection.

After visiting the church keep straight on. At the Mairie, of which only the front remains standing, *turn to the right into the Rue Boucton-Fayréaux. Follow this street to the Place Gambetta (about 200 yards distant), where turn to the left.* The entrance to "Pommern Tunnel," which connected up the German rear and front lines (*photo, p. 163*), is in this square.

The German inscriptions in the tunnel have been taken down, and the entrance blocked up, on account of the roof and walls giving way.

ENTRANCE TO "POMMERN TUNNEL" AT WITRY-LES-REIMS

Leaving the Place Gambetta, take the Rheims-Rethel road (*N.* 51) *on the left, then the first street on the right to the* **Fort of Witry.**

Just outside the village the road crosses the old Roman causeway from Rheims to Treves, *and a little further on passes to the left of the* **Fort of Witry.**

The **Fort of Witry** suffered but little from the bombardments.

The road climbs the northern slopes of the Berru Hill, across numerous German trenches. *At the bottom of a short run-down, opposite the village of Berru, is a crossing of four ways. The road leading to the fort is the one straight ahead.*

On the right, among the numerous defences, is a German cemetery containing a monument to the dead, ornamented with somewhat rudimentary carving and bearing an epitaph dedicated to the memory of the German soldiers who fell in the battles around Rheims.

The road continues up the slopes of Berru Hill, to the right of the way leading to the auxiliary battery of the fort of **Vigie de Berru.** *The top of the hill is soon reached,* on which the fort, known as the "Vigie de Berru," stands. This fort was little bombarded, and is practically intact.

Berru Hill, on account of its height, its sulphurous and ferruginous waters, flint quarries, and fertile soil, was inhabited in pre-historic times. At the summit, a *campignien* workshop, and farther down, above the springs which supply the village with water, a neolithic station have been discovered. Thousands of knives, arrow-heads, scrapers, saws, and other primitive tools have been unearthed. In the Gallo-Roman times the village must have been fairly important, judging by the vestiges of the ancient buildings discovered at the foot of the hill. It was near Berru that the *Gaulish helmet,* now in the National Museum of St. Germain, was found. Towards the end of the 16th century (about 1575), during the Leaguers' struggles around Rheims, the village was fortified, to protect it from pillaging by the soldiers. The moats and glacis which surrounded it are still visible to the south, where, covered with trees, they adjoin the gardens. Subterranean places of refuge, the entrance to which is no longer known, formerly existed underneath the village.

From the fort, the road winds down the opposite slopes of the hill. At the bottom of the latter, leave on the right the road to the **Fort of Nogent l'Abbesse,** *seen on the high ground to the right.*

ENTRANCE TO BEINE VILLAGE BY THE ROAD TO NOGENT L'ABBESSE

Nogent l'Abesse—Beine—Berru

(*See Itinerary, p.* 160, *and summary of the Military Operations, p* 154.)

The village of **Nogent l'Abbesse** *is next reached, at the entrance to which the road divides into three branches. Take the middle one* (*G.C.* 64), *which leads to the* ruined village of **Beine.** *During the run-down to the village, there is* a fine view of the Champagne Hills in front (Mont Cornillet and Mont Haut).

The village of **Beine** was one of the oldest demesnes belonging to the Abbey of St. Remi-de-Reims. It was made into a *commune* at the end of the 12th century.

The church of St. Laurent, situated in the centre of the village, was an excellent specimen of the transition style of the 12th century (*photo below*).

A road leading to Sillery leaves Beine in a south-westerly direction, but owing to its bad condition it is impossible to use it for returning to Rheims. The

RUINS OF THE CHURCH AT BEINE

BERRU CHURCH

trenches and shell holes have barely been filled in, and the temporary bridges over the wider trenches would probably break down under a fairly heavy car. On the other hand, the huge craters made by the Germans in the course of their retreat, have only been summarily repaired and are not practicable for motor-cars. *Tourists should therefore return to Nogent l'Abbesse by the road they came by.*

Enter the village by the main street, which follow as far as the church, whose belfry has been destroyed.

After the church, take the first street on the right, then the second road on the left (*G.C.* 64), *which leads to* **Berru.** *In front of the village, turn to the left and cross straight through.* The 12th century Church of St. Martin, which suffered only slightly from the bombardments, *is in the middle of the village, on the left* (*photo above*).

On leaving Berru, the tourist comes again to the crossing mentioned on p. 163. *Turn to the right and return to Witry-les-Reims by the road previously followed.*

At Witry-les-Reims, take N. 51 *on the left, passing by the* ruined works of Linguet (*photo below*).

Rheims is reached by the Faubourg Cérès. Keep straight on to the Place Royale, via the Rue du Faubourg Cérès and the Rue Cérès.

RUINS OF THE LINGUET WORKS

SECOND DAY

AFTERNOON

LA POMPELLE FORT—SILLERY

(*See complete Itinerary, p.* 121.)

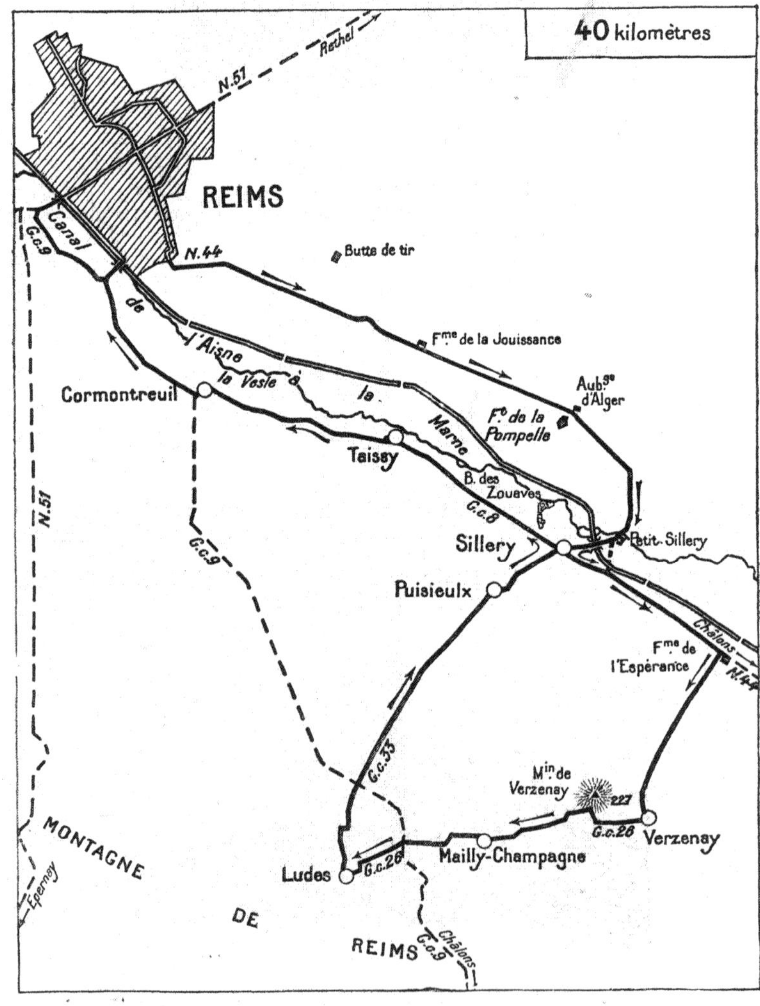

This Itinerary will take the tourist through two regions of entirely different characters.

The first part is devoted to visiting the battlefield south-east of Rheims, which was the scene of much desperate fighting throughout the war, but especially in 1918. This region formed the pivot of the French right wing, and remained firm despite the repeated powerful attacks of the enemy.

The second part of the Itinerary leaves the battlefield proper, and conducts the tourist across the most reputed vine-growing centres of Champagne (Verzenay, Mailly-Champagne and Ludes), through lovely, picturesque country, which, although it has somewhat suffered from the bombardments, has nevertheless retained its per-war aspect.

Leave Rheims by the Avenue de Châlons, continued by N. 44 (*see the plan of Rheims between pp.* 32 *and* 33, *F.* 6 *and H.* 7).

The Avenue de Châlons was well within the first-line defences.

Two communicating trenches run along the footpaths on either side of the Avenue.

Skirt Pommery Park, *on the left,* completely ravaged by the bombardment and the net-work of trenches which cross it.

As soon as the last houses of the town have been left behind, the tourist finds himself in the midst of the battlefield.

The sector, known as **"La Butte-de-Tir,"** situated on the left, below Cernay and beyond the railway, was the scene of furious fighting throughout the German occupation of 1914 to 1918 (*photo below*).

THE "BUTTE-DE-TIR" SECTOR

Listening-post in front of Cernay village.

COMMUNICATING TRENCH AT JOUISSANCE FARM (1915)

The road crosses the Châlons Railway (*l.c.*), *and goes thence direct to the* **Fort of La Pompelle,** passing through an inextricable network of trenches and barbed wire entanglements. The country hereabouts was completely ravaged by the terrific bombardments, and recalls the devastated regions around Verdun, near Vaux and Douaumont (*see the Michelin Illustrated Guide : Verdun, and the Battles for its Possession*).

La Jouissance Farm is next passed. Nothing remains either of it or of the road, *which started from this point towards Cernay, on the left.*

LA POMPELLE FORT (1918)

THE MOATS OF LA POMPELLE FORT (1918)

The **Fort of La Pompelle,** *which is next reached,* is now a mere heap of ruins. The road which led to the fort no longer exists. *To visit the ruins of the fort, tourists will have to follow on foot the narrow-gauge railway which starts from the road (photo above).*

Tradition has it that St. Timothy came from Asia to convert Rheims, suffered martyrdom, together with St. Apollinaris and several companions, on the hill known as *La Pompelle,* so-called perhaps from the procession (*pompa* or *pompella*) which, in the Middle Ages, used to visit the place of martyrdom of the saints.

This hill, which rises close to the crossing of the Rheims-St.-Hilaire-le-Grand and Rheims-Châlons Roads, was fortified after 1870, to flank the position of Berru on the south.

The road from Rheims to Saint-Hilaire-le-Grand (*G.C.* 7), which used to start from the "Alger Inn," at the cross-roads mentioned above, no longer exists. Like the inn, it was obliterated by the shelling. A huge crater now occupies the site of the Alger Inn (*photo below*).

CRATER, WHERE USED TO STAND THE "ALGER INN"

THE IMMEDIATE VICINITY OF WHAT WAS THE "ALGER INN" (1918)

Continue along N. 44. *About* 1 *kilometre from the fort, at a bend in the road,* the shattered remnants of trees of an avenue are visible on the left. Under the first fir-tree of this avenue, about 20 yards from the national road, is an armoured machine-gun shelter, almost intact.

Cross the railway (*l.c.*) *near the entirely destroyed station of Petit-Sillery. After passing* a ruined château *on the left, cross the bridge over the Vesle. At the fork beyond the bridge, leave N.* 44 *and take G.C.* 8 *on the right to* **Sillery.**

This village, renowned for its dry wine, is pleasantly situated on the banks on the Vesle. Throughout the war, it was quite close to the trenches and was frequently bombarded. In May, 1916, only some fifty of its inhabitants remained in the village, which subsequently suffered very severely, especially in 1918.

Take a turn in the village, then follow N. 44 *towards Châlons* (*see Itinerary, p.* 166).

THE "PLACE DE LA MAIRIE" AT SILLERY (1918)

The region of **Sillery-Pompelle** was the scene of much fierce fighting throughout the war. After the capture of **La Pompelle** and the **"Alger Inn"** by the French 10th Corps on the night of September 17–18, 1914, the Germans increased the number of their attacks, with a view to regaining these important positions.

One of these attacks (that of December 30, 1914) was preceded by the explosion of a mine at the "Alger Inn," which made a hole 130 feet in diameter by 55 feet deep (*see photo, p.* 169). After a hand-to-hand fight, the French drove back the enemy and remained masters of the crater.

In 1918, during their offensives against Rheims, the Germans attacked several times in this region. On June 1, between **Pommery Park** (in the south-eastern outskirts of Rheims) and the north-east of Sillery, they attacked with eight or nine battalions and fifteen tanks. The garrison of Fort Pompelle, momentarily encircled, held out until a furious counter-attack by the French Colonial Infantry relieved it and drove back the assailants. The German tanks were either captured or destroyed. On the 18th, after an hour's intense bombardment, the Germans made a fresh attack and secured a footing in the Northern Cemetery of Rheims and in the north-eastern outskirts of Sillery, but French counter-attacks drove them out almost immediately. From July 15 to 17 their attacks on Sillery were likewise repulsed.

Continue along N. 44 *to the* destroyed Espérance Farm (*about* 2 *kilometres distant*), *then turn to the right.* Numerous military works were made by the French in the embankments of the Aisne-Marne canal along the left side of the road.

The road rises towards the "Mountain of Rheims." A white tower, dominating the whole plain, *is seen on the left* (*photo below*).

Verzenay *is next reached by the Rue de Sillery.*

VERZENAY, SEEN FROM THE VERZENAY—MAILLY—CHAMPAGNE ROAD

THE OLD MILL AT VERZENAY

It was at **Verzenay** that, on the evening of September 3, 1914, the German aeroplane, which had dropped bombs on Rheims the same morning, was brought down. It has suffered relatively little from the bombardments.

To visit the church, which contains the tomb of Saint-Basle (*chapel on the right*), *take the Rue Gambetta, then the Rue Thiers.*

After visiting the church, return to the Rue Thiers, at the end of which is the Rue de Mailly (*G.C.* 26).

Take the latter, which, on leaving Verzenay, rises fairly stiffly.

At the top of the hill, on the right, begins the road leading to **Verzenay Mill,** which crowns Hill 227 (*see Itinerary, p.* 166, *and photo above*).

This mill, whence there is a fine panorama of the plain as far as the hills of Berru and Moronvilliers, was a military observation-post of the first order during the siege warfare.

It belongs to the champagne-wine firm of Heidsick Monopole, which allows tourists to visit it, as also their vineyards in the surrounding country.

The road dips down to Mailly-Champagne, *at the entrance to which village turn to the right into the Rue Gambetta, then to the left into the Rue de Ludes* (*G.C.* 26). The road, cut out of the hillside, is very picturesque as far as Ludes. In the forest, on the left of the road, are numerous "*cendrières,*" or quarries, from which volcanic sulphurous cinders, used for improving the vines, are extracted. Heaps of these valuable cinders (grey, white and black) are frequently encountered at the side of the road.

Ludes *is next reached by the Avenue de la Gare.*

The region just passed through, including the villages of Verzenay, Mailly-Champagne and Ludes, as well as Verzy (*to the east*), and Rilly-la-Montagne and Villers-Allerand (*to the west*), are the wine-growing centres of the "Mountain of Rheims" properly so-called, the black grapes from which produce the best brands of Champagne. The villages are picturesquely situated at the edge of the forests which crown the hills, while the vineyards which cover the slopes of the latter descend to the chalky plain. These vineyards, divided into tiny plots, the ground of which before the ravages of the phylloxera cost as much as 93,000 francs per hectare (about 2½ acres), constitute the principal wealth of the country. Here and there they have suffered from the war, but this has not prevented the vine-dressers from cultivating them (often with the help of the soldiers) or from gathering the grapes, under the continual menace of the German guns.

PUISIEULX. THE CHURCH AND ROAD TO SILLERY

At **Ludes,** in the *Avenue de la Gare, turn to the right into the Rue de Cormontreuil, and again to the right, into the Rue de Puisieulx* (*G.C.* 33).

At the crossing, 1 *kilometre beyond Ludes, go straight on. After passing on the right an avenue bordered with trees leading to the* **Château of Romont, Puisieulx** *is reached.*

At the first crossing, on entering the village, keep straight on, then turn to the right as far as the ruined church, with its curious loop-holed chevet. *Leave the church on the right and, at the end of the village, turn to the left.* There are a few graves *on the right of the road. After skirting a large estate, the trees of which were destroyed by shell-fire, the tourist reaches* **Sillery.**

RUINED CHURCH OF TAISSY

Turn to the left into G.C. 8, at the entrance to the village. On the right are vestiges of a small wood, known as "Zouaves Wood," which was the scene of many sanguinary fights after its capture by the French in 1914.

The tourist next reaches **Taissy**, whose ruined church *is on the right, by the side of the Vesle* (*photo, p. 173*).

This interesting church is largely Romanesque in style (tower, chevet and nave). The tabernacle, with altar-piece of carved wood, is Louis XIII. A fine wrought-iron railing encloses the sanctuary (*photo below*). The small, sonorous bell of the belfry is, strange to say, 13th or 14th century.

Pass straight through Taissy, then follow the tram-lines. **Cormontreuil** *is entered by the Rue Victor-Hugo.*

From Cormontreuil, the tourist may return to Rheims either by turning to the right in the village, beyond the tram station (in this case he will enter Rheims by the Rue de Cormontreuil which leads to the Place Dieu-Lumière) or by continuing straight ahead. In the latter case he will cross the Faubourg Fléchambault by the Rue Ledru-Rollin. At the end of the latter, turn to the right into the Rue Fléchambault which, after crossing the Vesle and the canal, leads to the Church of St. Remi.

THE CHOIR OF TAISSY CHURCH

CONTENTS

	PAGES
Political History of Rheims	3–7
Military History of Rheims	8 and 9
The Battles for Rheims, 1914–1918	9–15
The Destruction of Rheims by the bombardments	16–21
Life in the bombarded City	21–26
I.—A VISIT TO THE CITY	27–120
THE CATHEDRAL (description of)	28–60
History of the Cathedral	28–30
The Cathedral during the War	31 and 32
Coloured Plan of Rheims	between 32 and 33
Plan of the Cathedral and Archi-episcopal Palace	33
Exterior of the Cathedral	34–49
Interior of the Cathedral	50–60
FIRST ITINERARY—THE CITY	61–94
The Place du Parvis	62
The Archi-episcopal Palace	63–66
The Place Drouet d'Erlon and The Promenades	70 and 71
The Hôtel-de-Ville	72
The Place des Marchés	74
The Place Royale	78
The Musicians' House	80
The Mars Gate	82
The Rue de Cérès	87
SECOND ITINERARY—THE CITY (*continued*)	95–120
The Rue Chanzy	95–97
The Lycée	97 and 98
The Abbey of Saint Pierre-les-Dames	98
The Pommery Wine-Cellars	101
The Church of St. Remi	103–116
The Hôtel-Dieu (Hospital)	117

THE RUE DE LA GRUE, SEEN FROM THE RUE CÉRÈS

II.—A Visit to the Battlefield.

PAGES

First Itinerary (Morning) 122-133
Ormes 124
St. Euphraise 127
Coulommes-la-Montagne 128
Gueux 129
Thillois 131

cond Itinerary (Afternoon) 134-159
Tinqueux 135
Merfy 137
St. Thierry 138
Villers-Franqueux 141
Cormicy 144
Le Godat 148
Loivre 150
Brimont 152
The "Cavaliers de Courcy" 156
La Neuvillette 158

Third Itinerary (Morning) 160-165
Bourgogne—Fresnes 161
Witry-les-Reims 162
Nogent l'Abesse—Beine—Berru 164

Fourth Itinerary (Afternoon) 166-174
The Butte-de-Tir 167
The Fort de la Pompelle 168
Alger Inn 169
Verzenay 172

HERMONVILLE PORCH

www.ingramcontent.com/pod-product-compliance
Ingram Content Group UK Ltd.
Pitfield, Milton Keynes, MK11 3LW, UK
UKHW041847190726
13854UKWH00002B/758

9 781843 420675